OSPREY COMBAT AIRCRAFT • 74

JUNKERS Ju 87
STUKAGESCHWADER
OF THE
RUSSIAN FRONT

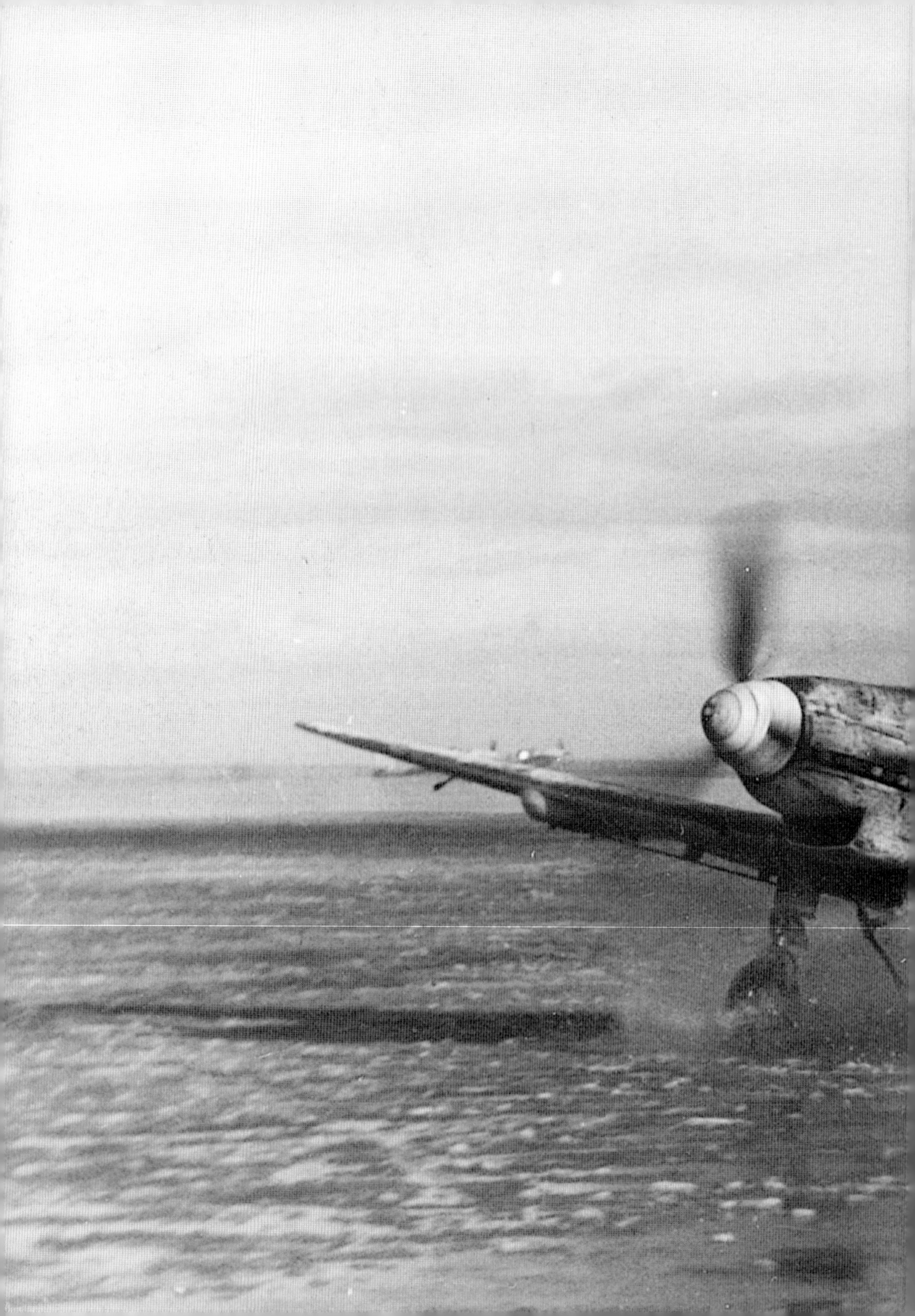

SERIES EDITOR: TONY HOLMES

OSPREY COMBAT AIRCRAFT • 74

JUNKERS Ju 87 *STUKAGESCHWADER* OF THE RUSSIAN FRONT

JOHN WEAL

OSPREY
PUBLISHING

Front cover
The epic battle of Stalingrad, which ended in the annihilation of Germany's 6. *Armee*, is rightly seen by many as the turning point of the war in the east. Apart from an unfortunate minority, however, the men of the Stuka units that had accompanied General Friedrich von Paulus' troops during their advance on the city escaped the fate that befell a quarter of a million of their ground comrades. The *Stukagruppen* were withdrawn long before the struggle for Stalingrad reached its climax. Only a single *Sonderstaffel* (Special squadron) of Ju 87s continued to operate from within the Stalingrad pocket. Throughout its seven-week existence, this *Staffel* was commanded by Leutnant Heinz Jungclaussen, the *Kapitän* of 6./StG 2 'Immelmann'.

Mark Postlethwaite's striking cover illustration captures Jungclaussen's winter-camouflaged 'Anton-Paula' as it commences its dive on a target near the 'Red October' iron works just to the north of the distinctive rail loop that was known to every German fighting in the city as the 'tennis racquet'.

Jungclaussen went on to add another 800 Stuka missions to the 200 he had flown over Stalingrad before becoming an instructor in early 1944. He returned to operations in November of that year as a *Schlacht* pilot on the western front, flying Fw 190s as the *Staffelkapitän* of 3./SG 4, only to be killed in action against RAF Typhoons over the Rhine south of Koblenz on 26 December 1944 (*Cover artwork by Mark Postlethwaite*)

First published in Great Britain in 2008 by Osprey Publishing
Midland House, West Way, Botley, Oxford, OX2 0PH
44-02 23rd St, Suite 219, Long Island City, NY 11101, USA
E-mail – info@ospreypublishing.com

© 2008 Osprey Publishing Limited

All rights reserved. Apart from any fair dealing for the purpose of private study, research, criticism or review, as permitted under the Copyright, Design and Patents Act 1988, no part of this publication may be reproduced, stored in a retrieval system, or transmitted in any form or by any means, electronic, electrical, chemical, mechanical, optical, photocopying, recording or otherwise without prior written permission. All enquiries should be addressed to the publisher.

ISBN: 978 1 84603 308 7

CIP Data for this publication is available from the British Library

Edited by Tony Holmes
Page design by Tony Truscott
Cover Artwork by Mark Postlethwaite
Aircraft Profiles by John Weal
Index by Alan Thatcher
Originated by PDQ Digital Media Solutions
Printed and bound in China through Bookbuilders

09 10 11 12 13   11 10 9 8 7 6 5 4 3 2

FOR A CATALOGUE OF ALL BOOKS PUBLISHED BY OSPREY MILITARY AND AVIATION PLEASE CONTACT:

Osprey Direct, c/o Random House Distribution Center,
400 Hahn Road, Westminster, MD 21157
Email: uscustomerservice@ospreypublishing.com

Osprey Direct, The Book Service Ltd, Distribution Centre, Colchester Road, Frating Green, Colchester, Essex, CO7 7DW
E-mail: customerservice@ospreypublishing.com

www.ospreypublishing.com

ACKNOWLEDGEMENTS
The author wishes to thank the following individuals for their generous help in providing information and photographs – Thomas Bryant, Manfred Griehl, Heinrich, Walter Matthiesen, Chris Pavitt, Dr Alfred Price and Robert Simpson. Among the many ex-Stuka personnel who gave of their time and help in the past, but who are no longer with us, the author would particularly like to mention a friend of more than 50 years standing, Rolf Hase of the *Gruppenstab* II./StG 2 'Immelmann', who sadly passed away while this work was in preparation.

CONTENTS

CHAPTER ONE
1941 – LAST *BLITZKRIEG* 6

CHAPTER TWO
1942 – ROAD TO ARMAGEDDON 30

CHAPTER THREE
1943 – YEAR OF REORGANISATION 64

CHAPTER FOUR
1941-45 – ALLIES COME AND ALLIES GO 78

CHAPTER FIVE
1944-45 – *PANZER*-BUSTING POSTSCRIPT 86

APPENDICES 88
COLOUR PLATES COMMENTARY 92
INDEX 95

1941 – LAST BLITZKRIEG

CHAPTER ONE

The fearsome reputation of the Junkers Ju 87 Stuka dive-bomber was established during the first two *Blitzkrieg* campaigns of World War 2, namely the attack on Poland and the invasion of the Low Countries and France. It was only after the successful conclusion of the latter, when the Luftwaffe crossed the Channel to take the air war into the skies of southern England, that the Stuka's inherent faults were laid bare. Lacking sufficient speed and defensive power, it was simply unable to survive in airspace defended by a determined and organised enemy.

Withdrawn from operations at the height of the Battle of Britain, the bent-wing Junkers was rarely to be seen again by daylight in northwest Europe. Yet it was to enjoy a new lease of life far to the south. In the Balkans campaign, in the airborne invasion of Crete, in anti-shipping missions against naval vessels and merchant convoys in the Mediterranean and in the early stages of the desert conflict in North Africa – all areas where enemy air opposition was at first woefully inadequate – the Stuka regained something of its myth as a successful weapon of war. But here too, once Allied air superiority had been achieved, the Junkers' failings were all too apparent.

By the time hostilities in the Mediterranean theatre drew to a close, the Luftwaffe's Stuka force comprised just two dozen or so machines operating solely under the cover of darkness (for details of the Ju 87's earlier combat career in Spain, Poland, the West and in the Mediterranean, see *Osprey Combat Aircraft Nos 1 and 6*).

And there was another battlefront where the same sorry saga of the Stuka was, it seemed, about to be played out for yet a third time – the initial spectacular successes, followed by the inexorable growth of enemy air opposition, and then the inevitable relegation to night operations. But in Russia things were to prove different. Armed with a pair of 37 mm cannon underwing, the Ju 87 enjoyed a new lease of life as a specialised anti-tank aircraft. And on the eastern front at least – albeit in relatively small numbers – the Stuka would remain in action by day until war's end.

Operation *Barbarossa*, Germany's invasion of the Soviet Union on 22 June 1941, was the last and most ambitious *Blitzkrieg* of them all. But despite the enormity of the undertaking, such were the Luftwaffe's commitments elsewhere by that summer of 1941 – the defence of the occupied western territories and the fighting in the Mediterranean – that it launched the attack on Russia with far fewer aircraft than had been available to it for the assault on France and the Low Countries in the spring of the previous year.

The disparity between Stuka strengths on the eves of the two invasions was particularly striking. One source quotes the number of serviceable

In the beginning, during the opening rounds of *Barbarossa*, the Stukas again enjoyed mastery of the air much as they had done during the earlier French and Polish campaigns. Here, a *Staffel* wings its way unescorted and unmolested high above the featureless Russian landscape

This *Kette* of Ju 87Bs lifting off for another raid on Soviet positions arouses little more than casual interest from a couple of onlookers. The amount of ordnance scattered about in the foreground would seem to indicate that there is little fear of enemy retaliation

The small fires quickly taking hold in the tinder-dry fields and scrubland below suggest that this attack is being carried out either with anti-personnel bombs or clusters of incendiaries

Ju 87s deployed in readiness for the *Blitzkrieg* in the west as having been 301. The comparable figure for *Barbarossa* is given as just 183 (with a further 24 up in the far north above the Arctic Circle).

The main assault force of Stukas – seven *Gruppen* in total – all came under the command of *Luftflotte* 2 on the central sector of the front. They were divided between the air fleet's two *Fliegerkorps*. Subordinated to VIII. *Fliegerkorps* on the left, or northern, flank of the sector were *Stab* StG 1 with II. and III./StG 1, plus *Stab* StG 2 with I. and III./StG 2. On the right, or southern, flank under II. *Fliegerkorps* were all three *Gruppen* of StG 77.

The task of the two *Fliegerkorps'* Stuka units was to support the armoured divisions of *Panzergruppen* 3 and 2 respectively as they drove eastwards in a series of giant pincer movements towards their ultimate goal – Moscow.

Accounts of the opening day of *Barbarossa* are nearly always dominated by the astronomical scores achieved by the Luftwaffe's fighters both in the air and on the ground. Some 325 Soviet aircraft were shot down on 22 June 1941, the vast majority of them falling to Bf 109s. The German *Jagdgruppen* were also responsible for a sizeable proportion of the nearly 1500 Red Air Force machines destroyed on the ground, either by low-level strafing or by dropping hundreds of the devilish little 2-kg SD 2 'butterfly bombs'.

A number of Stukas also flew missions on this day armed with the 'butterfly bomb's' larger counterpart, the 10-kg SD 10 anti-personnel bomb. These were carried in underwing containers and dropped indiscriminately on enemy airfields and known troop concentrations. But such scattergun tactics were a waste of the Ju 87's unique capabilities, and during the early morning hours of 22 June most Stukas were employed in their more traditional role delivering precise attacks on pinpoint targets. III./StG 1, for example, was ordered to knock out three Red Army HQ buildings at dawn;

'As each aircraft's engine sprang into life, its dispersal pen was fitfully illuminated by the flickering flames from the exhaust stubs. Red, green and white lights wove through the darkness as the machines taxied to their assigned take-off positions.

'The three aircraft of the HQ flight lifted off together at 0230 hrs, leaving a thick cloud of dust in their wake. Despite their total lack of visibility, those following all got off safely. One by one, they emerged from the dust cloud, their position lights indicating their passage as they closed up on the leaders until the *Gruppe* formation was complete. In the pale half-light of pre-dawn, villages, roads and railway lines could just be made out through the layers of mist blanketing the ground.'

III./StG 1 was to have rendezvoused with II. *Gruppe* before entering Russian airspace, but the two units failed to link up. After circling for a few minutes, Hauptmann Helmut Mahlke, the *Gruppenkommandeur* of III./StG 1, assumed – quite rightly, as it turned out – that Hauptmann Anton Keil's II. *Gruppe* must have gone on ahead. He set out after them;

'We crossed the border – a peculiar feeling. A new theatre of war, a new foe, but at first all remained quiet. The Soviets appeared to be fast asleep! The first bombs from II./StG 1 detonate some way off in front of us. Then it's our turn. A few stray puffs of smoke blossom in the sky. The enemy flak has finally woken up. But the gunners' aim is so wild and uncertain that old Stuka hands such as ourselves pay it little heed.

'The pilots have spotted their targets. Attack! We dive almost vertically, one after the other in quick succession. In a few seconds it's all over. The ruins of the HQ buildings are shrouded in dust, smoke and flames. We get back into formation and head for home.'

Still bearing the fuselage codes associated with their previous identity (see the colour plates commentary for Profile 2 on page 92), these two machines of II./StG 1 make their way back to base after the completion of another successful mission

The *Gruppe* landed back at Dubovo-South at 0348 hrs, its first mission in-theatre having lasted just 78 minutes. Just under two hours later the aircrews set out again. This time their job was to block the approaches to the bridge spanning the River Niemen at Grodno to prevent its being blown up by the Russians. This second operation was also successful. The Grodno bridge – a potential bottleneck on *Panzergruppe* 3's planned advance on Minsk, capital of white Russia – was saved from demolition and III./StG 1 again returned to base without loss.

Three more missions were flown before the day was out, two of them safeguarding further important river crossing points. The last Stuka touched down back at Dubovo-South at 2108 hrs – five operations in just under 19 hours – with the next take-off scheduled for 0330 hrs the following morning! But such was to be the norm rather than the exception during the opening rounds of *Barbarossa*, with all the other Stuka units being worked equally as hard. On StG 1's immediate left, the two *Gruppen* of Major Oskar Dinort's StG 2 'Immelmann' spent the entire 22 June ceaselessly pounding away at the Soviet frontier defences to the east and southeast of Suwalki.

Meanwhile, in II. *Fliegerkorps'* sector, StG 77's three *Gruppen* were engaged in smashing a breach through the Red Army's fortified positions along the line of the River Bug. This was the jumping-off area for *Panzergruppe* 2's advance eastwards along the northern edge of the Pripyet Marshes. It was here that the Soviet air force seemed to rally more quickly than elsewhere along the front. Back at their bases between missions, the Stukas of StG 77 themselves became the targets for constant waves of enemy bombers. But the unescorted Tupolevs were hacked down in droves by the defending fighters of JG 51. At Byala Podlaska alone, one pilot of II./StG 77 reported seeing 21 bombers crash nearby. Not one Stuka was damaged.

In fact, on the opening day of *Barbarossa* only two Ju 87s were lost to enemy action (and a third damaged from other causes) along the entire 170-mile (270 km) stretch of the central sector from the Rivel Memel down to the Pripyet.

Within 24 hours the armoured spearheads of *Panzergruppen* 2 and 3 were through the Soviets' rapidly disintegrating frontier defences and racing for Minsk. Most Stuka units now reverted to their more usual role of 'flying artillery', supporting the German armies in the field by blasting the way clear ahead of them, and preventing the enemy from mounting counter-attacks by disrupting his lines of communication and supply.

On the northern flank of the central sector, for example, 23 June found the Ju 87s of VIII. *Fliegerkorps* attacking – among other objectives – rail targets 90 miles (150 km) inside enemy territory. StG 1 destroyed a number of trains carrying guns and light tanks along the stretch of line from Vilna (Vilnius), near the Lithuanian border, down to the important junction at Lida, while StG 2 targeted stations and marshalling yards, including that at Volkovisk, between Bialystok and Minsk.

On the southern flank, however, there was an added complication. Although the leading elements of *Panzergruppe* 2 were already well on their way towards Minsk, the frontier fortress citadel of Brest-Litovsk was still holding out. It posed a significant and ongoing threat to the Germans' own main supply route, which passed within range of the fortress's heavy guns.

CHAPTER ONE

Bridges would feature high on the Stukas' list of targets throughout the war on the eastern front. Having demolished the road bridge in the background, this unit – note the Ju 87 pulling up and away at top right – was recalled several days later to destroy the pontoon bridge the Soviets had constructed to replace it

The capture of the citadel had therefore become a priority. But its metre-thick walls proved impervious to artillery and mortar bombardment, and StG 77 was called upon to do its job. Yet not even the Stukas could pound the stubborn defenders into submission.

A weeklong bombardment culminated in the entire *Geschwader* – very nearly 100 Ju 87s in all – being despatched against the citadel's east fort on the morning of 29 June. Although numerous direct hits were scored, the Junkers' 600-kg (1100-lb) bombs had little effect. That afternoon a *Staffel* of twin-engined Ju 88s carrying 1800-kg (4000-lb) 'Satan' bombs was sent in and Soviet resistance was finally broken.

Meanwhile, 24 June had seen the first four Knight's Crosses awarded to Stuka pilots serving on the eastern front. The recipients, however, all members of StG 2 (see Appendix 2), were not being honoured for their actions against the Soviets over the last 48 hours, but for their previous exploits – primarily on anti-shipping operations – during the recent Greek and Cretan campaigns.

Bombs already loaded, *'Bertas'* of StG 77 run up their engines at dispersal prior to taxiing out for another strike on the Soviet fortress at Brest-Litovsk in June 1941

It was also on 24 June that III./StG 1 fell foul of Russian fighters. The *Gruppe* had already flown two missions that day without incident, but during the third (a raid on the northern outskirts of Minsk) it was attacked by half-a-dozen I-16s. The Soviet pilots claimed six Stukas shot down, but III./StG 1's loss returns give details of only one victim – a 9. *Staffel* machine that went down in flames some 15 miles (25 km) northwest of Minsk. Another Ju 87, flown by *Gruppenkommandeur* Hauptmann Helmut Mahlke, was reportedly hit by quadruple flak and forced to land behind enemy lines. Mahlke and his gunner evaded capture and succeeded in returning to their unit three days later.

27 June was also the date on which *Panzergruppen* 2 and 3 closed the ring around Minsk when their leading armoured *Korps* – XXXXVII. from the south and LVII. from the north – linked up on the far side of the city. Over a third of a million enemy troops were trapped in the huge pocket, or 'cauldron', that stretched more than 220 miles (350 km) westwards from the white Russian capital back to Bialystok and beyond.

For the next 12 days, while Luftwaffe fighters blocked every attempt by Red Air Force bombers to blast open an escape route for their encircled armies, all seven of *Luftflotte 2*'s *Stukagruppen* hurled everything they had into the battle to annihilate the Minsk-Bialystok cauldron. From their landing grounds at Lyck and Praschnitz in East Prussia, the Ju 87s of I. and III./StG 2 attacked the northern perimeter of the elongated east-west pocket. And before the month was out, elements of StG 1 would be transferred down to Baranovichi to reinforce StG 77's operations over the southern half of the cauldron.

But whether north or south, the targets were the same – enemy troop movements, concentrations of armour, river crossings and railway lines. Yet amid all the mayhem and destruction there was still the odd moment of humour. On one occasion a small group of German troops fought their way across a railway bridge and gained a toehold on the enemy riverbank, only for the Soviets to bring up an armoured train. Pinned down by heavy fire, the infantry called for assistance from the Stukas.

A single *Staffel* duly arrived on the scene and began their work with clinical precision. The first two bombs cratered the railway embankment in front of and behind the train so that it was unable to move. Then the rest of the *Staffel* dived down to take out the train itself. This they accomplished in short order. But two pilots were baffled as to why their bombs exploded in a wood some distance away from the track. How could they have missed a sitting target – stationary, no defensive fire, no fighters in the vicinity, their bombs not released until almost on top of the middle wagon of the armoured behemoth – by such a wide margin?

Back at base, the *Staffelkapitän*, who had been observing the attack, put them out of their misery. They had indeed hit the middle wagon as intended, but their bombs had bounced off the domed cupola on its roof and described a graceful parabola through the air before coming down in the trees over a hundred metres away from the track!

Like the armoured train in its final moments, the Soviet forces in the Minsk-Bialystok pocket had nowhere to go. And so they more often than not stood their ground and sent up a wall of anti-aircraft and small-arms fire whenever the Stukas appeared. Losses among the *Gruppen* inevitably began to mount. One casualty was future Oak Leaves winner Oberleutnant Helmut Leicht of StG 77, who was shot down and severely wounded on 28 June during his first operation on the Russian front.

By 9 July, however, it was all over. The cauldron had been reduced and nearly 324,000 Soviet troops had been taken prisoner, together with 3332 armoured vehicles and 1809 artillery pieces either captured or destroyed. Even more importantly, perhaps, the first objective had been

It did not necessarily require a direct hit to knock out an armoured vehicle. This T-26 – one of the most numerous tanks deployed by the Red Army in the initial phase of the war in the east – has been completely disabled by a near miss from a Stuka bomb and is clearly not going anywhere

CHAPTER ONE

achieved. Minsk was the western terminus of the Moscow highway. And roughly halfway along this main artery, only some 230 miles (370 km) from the Soviet capital, lay the next great prize – Smolensk.

In fact, leading elements of the central sector's two *Panzergruppen* were already driving hard for Smolensk even before the fighting for the Minsk cauldron had ended. Smolensk itself was taken by motorised infantry on 16 July, while *Panzergruppe* 2's armoured units began a wide pincer movement which was to result in the encirclement and destruction of parts of three Soviet armies in another giant cauldron battle.

But the vastness of the territories being conquered and occupied was beginning to expose the Wehrmacht's – and, in particular, the Luftwaffe's – underlying weakness. It simply did not possess sufficient strength to accomplish all the tasks being demanded of it. And very soon the carefully structured fabric of the original *Barbarossa* plan, comprising three clearly delineated sectors, north, centre and south, with three separate objectives, Leningrad, Moscow and the Ukraine, respectively, would start to unravel. Or, more accurately, be picked apart by Hitler's interfering in his generals' conduct of the war.

It was a process that would result in the role of the eastern front Stukas gradually, but inexorably, changing from that of 'flying artillery' to one of 'mobile fire brigade'. In the months and years to come they would be shunted about with increasing frequency, initially in support of some new offensive or local attack but, as the tide of war turned, latterly in ever more desperate attempts to plug the gaps being torn all along the disintegrating fronts from the Baltic to the Black Sea.

The first unit to undergo such redeployment was Oberstleutnant Clemens *Graf* von Schönborn-Wiesentheid's StG 77, which had been transferred down to *Luftflotte* 4 on the southern sector in the first week of July. Up until this time the south had been by far the quietest of the three sectors. But now the German 11. *Armee* was preparing to advance eastwards out of Rumania towards Kiev, the capital of the Ukraine. The first major obstacles in its path were the River Dniester and the partially completed Stalin Line fortifications straggling along its eastern bank. It was in order to support the army's crossing of the Dniester at Mogilev-Podolsky that StG 77 had been seconded to *Luftflotte* 4, and it thereby became the first *Stukageschwader* to engage the Soviet forces on the southern sector.

Meanwhile, StGs 1 and 2 were helping the Panzers close the ring around the Smolensk cauldron on the central sector. On 14 July Oberstleutnant Oskar Dinort, the long-serving *Kommodore* of StG 2 'Immelmann', was awarded the Oak Leaves.

A celebrated flyer and one of the founding fathers of the Stuka arm, 'Onkel Oskar' Dinort was the first dive-bomber pilot of the war to receive this prestigious decoration. Among his many accomplishments was the development and introduction of the percussion rods to which he gave his name. *Dinortstäbe* were extensions attached to the noses of a Stuka's 50-kg underwing bombs – they were rarely fitted to the aircraft's main 500-kg bomb as there was too high a risk of their fouling the propeller when launched from the ventral yoke. The extensions prevented the bombs from burying themselves deep in the ground before exploding (for more details see *Osprey Combat Aircraft 6*, page 35).

The many moves from one forward landing ground to the next made the work of maintenance a nightmare. At least the summer sun is still shining brightly as this 'Berta' suffers the indignity of being stripped bare out in the open

The percussion rod fuses extending from the noses of the underwing bombs of this 7./StG 77 machine (foreground) are clearly visible as groundcrew prepare the aircraft for its next mission. The mechanic perched atop the engine cowling is checking the coolant level

Forty-eight hours later, on 16 July, the *Kommandeur* of III./StG 1, Hauptmann Helmut Mahlke, received the Knight's Cross. Like those of 24 June, this award was no doubt conferred primarily on the strength of Mahlke's successes in earlier campaigns. But his more recent experiences during the opening days of *Barbarossa* may also have been a factor, for since returning to his unit on 27 June, Mahlke had been shot down twice more. On 1 July, while supporting the bridgehead thrown across the River Beresina at Borisov, east of Minsk, he had again been brought down by ground fire behind enemy lines. And again he had made his way back to safety on foot. And then, exactly one week later, III./StG 1 was despatched to the aid of a handful of armoured vehicles of 17 *Panzerdivision* that were trapped in a village with a long column of Soviet tanks bearing down on them.

As the enemy tanks were strung out nose to tail along the country road, Mahlke ordered his pilots to attack individually. Some scored direct hits and several tanks exploded, whilst others came to a standstill with clouds of smoke pouring from them. Then, as one, the remainder wheeled to either left or right and tried to escape at high speed into the fields bordering the road. But those inviting and innocent looking meadows proved to be marshland. Tanks began disappearing up to their turrets;

'They sank so quickly into the swamp that we couldn't even count them properly – but there must have been at least 20 of them!'

The trapped Germans were not out of danger yet, however. More enemy tanks were approaching, and Mahlke's *Gruppe* quickly mounted a second mission. But this time the Soviet armour had air cover. Caught by an enemy fighter, the *Kommandeur's* machine went down with both inboard wing tanks on fire. Mahlke and his gunner managed to bail out, but the latter's parachute failed to open. Severely burned, Mahlke was subsequently picked up by a motorcycle patrol sent out by

17. *Panzerdivision*, the unit his *Gruppe* had been protecting.

One of Mahlke's NCO pilots, future Knight's Cross recipient Oberfeldwebel Wilhelm Joswig of 8./StG 1, had perhaps an even more fortunate escape. On 15 July he had had to make a forced landing near Smolensk after his Stuka was hit by flak. Joswig was captured by the Soviets, which as a rule meant either immediate execution or a one-way ticket to Siberia. Incredibly, Joswig was found alive and liberated by German troops six days later.

The fighting for the Smolensk pocket would last until 5 August. During that time StG 77 in the south continued to support the ground troops' advance into the Ukraine. On 26 July the *Geschwader's* strength was split between *Luftflotte* 4's two component *Korps*, with *Stab*, II. and III./StG 77 being assigned to V. *Fliegerkorps*, which was supporting the main drive on Kiev, and I./StG 77 being detached to serve under IV. *Fliegerkorps* operating along the Black Sea coastal belt.

On 30 July Hauptmann Helmut Bode's III./StG 77 carried out an attack on the quarters of Marshal Timoshenko, but the Commander-in-Chief of the Soviet West Front escaped unscathed. Thereafter, the Stukas of StG 77 resumed their more normal activities, assisting the ground troops of Army Group South in the reduction of the Uman pocket – a smaller version of the Minsk and Smolensk cauldrons that netted 'only' some 100,000+ prisoners – and supporting the crossings of the next major river barrier, the Dnepr, at Kremenchug and Dnepropetrovsk.

It was at this juncture, little more than a month into the campaign, that the Stukas on the eastern front were to be spread even more thinly. Late in July, *Luftflotte* 2 received orders from High Command that VIII. *Fliegerkorps* was to be transferred *en bloc* to the northern sector. These instructions could not be implemented immediately, however, as a dangerous build-up of Soviet strength in the Smolensk area was threatening operations there, and it had to be dealt with first.

But in the opening week of August the bulk of von Richthofen's VIII. *Fliegerkorps* was despatched northwards, leaving behind only a small cadre under Major Walter Hagen, the *Kommodore* of StG 1, on the central front. This meant, in effect, that the Stuka forces in Russia were now dispersed across all three sectors, with StG 2 in the north, StG 1 in the centre and StG 77 in the south.

In historical terms, the campaign on the northern sector is today almost solely remembered for the '900-day' siege of Leningrad. But this epic struggle had yet to begin (the ring around the Soviet Union's second city would not be effectively closed until the beginning of September). 'Onkel Oskar' Dinort's Stukas were therefore initially employed supporting the ground troops fighting on the lesser known fronts around Lake Ilmen, some 125 miles (200 km) to the south of Leningrad.

Ready to roll, the pilot and air-gunner of 7./StG 77's 'F1+MM' keep their canopies open to dissipate the heat of the burning sun. Note that this aircraft is not wearing the *Staffel's* distinctive 'Eagle's head' badge (see photograph on page 13)

Much of the middle two weeks of August was taken up by operations along the line of the River Lovat, which empties into Lake Ilmen from the south. In particular, the Ju 87s of StG 2 covered the crossing of the Lovat by the 'Death's Head' division (3. SS-*Panzergrenadier*) and its subsequent advance beyond the river. On one occasion, after attacking a wooden bridge spanning another waterway to the east of Lake Ilmen, one of Dinort's Stukas returned to its Ryelbitzi base with a metre-long piece of wooden planking impaled in its wing – thrown up by the force of the explosion just as the Junkers was pulling out of its dive low overhead.

But, inevitably, StG 2 was drawn into the fighting around Leningrad. After further supporting the ground forces on the Volkhov front, and mounting a number of attacks on the strategically important Moscow-Leningrad rail supply line, I. and III./StG 2 had, by the beginning of September, been moved up to Tyrkovo, some 100 miles (160 km) south-southwest of Leningrad. From here they flew numerous missions over the city itself and against its outer defences.

But their most spectacular successes were to be achieved against the Soviet Baltic Fleet, which had been withdrawn from its more westerly bases along the Baltic coast and was now holed up in Leningrad and Kronstadt – the latter being the main Soviet harbour fortress on the offshore island of Kotlin, 15 miles (24 km) out in the Gulf of Finland.

Kronstadt was the stage which launched the meteoric rise to fame of the man who was not only to become the Luftwaffe's most successful Stuka pilot, but also the most highly decorated member of the entire Wehrmacht. Despite having joined the Luftwaffe back in 1936 and undergone training as a dive-bomber pilot, Leutnant Hans-Ulrich Rudel had been transferred to the long-range reconnaissance arm prior to the outbreak of World War 2. He served in this role in the Polish campaign, before then being posted as adjutant to a training regiment. Rudel had put in several official requests in the interim to return to Stukas, but all had been turned down. It was not until the late summer of 1940 that he eventually succeeded, joining first I./StG 3 and then, after a further stint of training, I./StG 2.

By now an Oberleutnant, Rudel's passage was still far from smooth, however. His somewhat out of the ordinary lifestyle – he was a strict teetotaller and keep-fit fanatic, who would spend many off-duty hours

A *Stabsstaffel* reconnaissance machine captures I./StG 2's attack on the railway bridge over the River Volkhov 40 miles (64 km) north-northeast of Novgorod on 17 August 1941. Billowing smoke (right) climbs into the air from a direct hit

'Flak thick enough to walk on', was an oft-heard complaint by US bomber crews returning from raids on the Reich. The barrage put up by the Soviet Baltic Fleet to protect its main base at Kronstadt evidently came into the same category – although it does not seem to be bothering the lone Stuka (centre left) seen here trundling along above the scattered clouds

running around the perimeter track long before the term 'jogging' had even been coined! – did not exactly endear him to his fellow pilots. Nor did it sit well with his superiors, who were not quite sure what to do with him. He was not given the chance to fly operationally during the Balkan and Cretan campaigns. And it was not until the opening day of *Barbarossa* that he finally flew his first four operational missions.

Shortly after this Rudel was transferred as the *Gruppen*-TO, or technical officer, to III./StG 2. And it was thus as a member of Hauptmann Ernst-Siegfried Steen's *Gruppenstab* (HQ Flight) that Oberleutnant Rudel lifted off from Tyrkovo on 16 September 1941 to attack elements of the Soviet Baltic Fleet off Leningrad.

The kernel of the surviving Soviet naval forces trapped in the Gulf of Finland (the easternmost basin of the Baltic) was formed by the two elderly battleships *Marat* and *Oktyabrskaya Revolutsia*. Although launched three years before the outbreak of World War 1, these two 26,000-ton behemoths still packed a powerful punch, their main armament consisting of a dozen 12-inch (305 mm) guns in the four triple turrets. In addition to the battleships, the Baltic Fleet also had a handful of modern cruisers, including the *Kirov* and *Maksim Gorky* (the latter less than a year old), each mounting nine 7.1-inch (180 mm) guns, plus a number of destroyers.

These vessels were all employed to bombard German positions along the coast and around Leningrad. They posed a very real threat to German ground forces as they were constantly being moved about in response to whichever part of the Soviet land defences most urgently required the support of their 'devastating and accurate' gunfire. But, as a rule, the two ancient battleships were restricted to navigating in the deep-water channel between Leningrad and Kronstadt. And it was a reconnaissance sighting of the *Marat* in action that had led to the despatch of StG 2's Stukas from Tyrkovo.

Despite the bad weather conditions, the three machines of III./StG 2's *Gruppenstab* spotted the *Marat* through a gap in the clouds and dived to the attack. Hauptmann Steen's bomb was a near miss, but Oberleutnant Rudel hit the battleship's afterdeck and he reported seeing 'flames break out'. The Stukas' 500-kg (1100-lb) bombs were not heavy enough to inflict mortal damage, however, and the *Marat* survived the onslaught by the 30+ machines of StG 2 that had been sent out to find it. German intelligence did lose track of the vessel though, and for a few days there was speculation that it may indeed have been sunk.

On 21 September, a long-awaited delivery of 1000-kg (2200-lb) bombs arrived at Tyrkovo and, by chance, the next morning's regular reconnaissance flight discovered the *Marat* lying under repair in Kronstadt harbour. Once again, StG 2's two *Gruppen* were ordered to mount a

A kapok life-jacketed crewman (foreground right) helps a pair of armourers prepare a 1000-kg (2200 lb) bomb for transfer from its wooden sled to the aircraft in the background while his Oberleutnant crew-mate looks on with a certain air of trepidation. The raincoats worn by the two armourers would seem to rule out the fact that this photograph was taken as StG 2 readied their aircraft for the legendary Kronstadt mission of 23 September – a day that by all accounts dawned 'fine and clear'

An enlargement of the reconnaissance photograph showing the damaged *Marat* (arrowed) berthed stern on to the head of one of Kronstadt's inner moles . . .

maximum effort against the ex-Czarist battleship. Unlike the weather on the earlier mission, 23 September dawned fine and clear, the sky a brilliant blue without a trace of cloud. The Stukas, led by *Geschwaderkommodore* Oberstleutnant Oskar Dinort, had to run a gauntlet of Soviet fighters and heavy anti-aircraft fire to reach their target.

On this occasion, the *Gruppenstab* of III./StG 2 consisted of just two machines – those flown by the *Kommandeur*, Hauptmann Steen, and his TO, Hans-Ulrich Rudel. The latter takes up the story;

'Steen and I maintain a steady course through the flak, telling ourselves that *Ivan* is not aiming at individual aircraft, but simply putting up a box barrage in our path. Other machines are weaving about all over the place, however, their pilots no doubt convinced that by zig-zagging and changing height they are making the gunners' task more difficult. As we approach Kronstadt there is little semblance of formation left. We are flying in an untidy gaggle, and the risk of mid-air collision is high.

'We are still several kilometres from our target, but off to one side ahead of me I can already make out the *Marat* berthed in the harbour. The Kronstadt flak is deadly, bursting in livid flashes of colour before dissipating into smudges of dirty smoke. From our height of 2750 m (9000 ft) I look down on the *Marat*. Moored behind her is the cruiser *Kirov*. Neither ship has opened up at us. We know from previous experience that they hold their fire until we are committed to the dive.

'Suddenly Steen tips on to one wing and starts to dive. I immediately follow suit and we hurtle downwards side-by-side at an angle approaching 80 degrees. I already have the *Marat* firmly in my sights. As she grows in size I can clearly make out the pinpricks of light from her many anti-aircraft guns. But what's this? Steen's aircraft is suddenly pulling ahead of me. He has retracted his dive-brakes in order to shorten the time taken in the dive and reduce the risk of being hit by enemy fire.

'Once again I follow his lead, retracting my own dive-brakes and going flat out after him. I quickly find myself right on his tail, travelling much too fast but completely unable to check my speed. Straight ahead of me I can see the expression of horror on the face of Steen's rear gunner. He's clearly expecting my propeller to chew the tail off their machine at any second!

'I push hard on the stick with all the strength I have in a desperate effort to increase the angle of my dive even more. I must now be going down almost vertically! But can I avoid Steen's aircraft, which is now right above my cockpit? I race past beneath him, missing him by a hair's breadth.

'My Ju 87 remains rock steady in its dive and the *Marat* begins to loom large in front of my eyes. I can even see sailors scurrying about on her deck. I press the bomb release switch and then heave back on the stick with all my might. Will I be able to pull out of the dive in time? I doubt it. In any case, I am now less than 300 metres (1000 ft) above the target, and we were told at briefing not to release our bombs below 1000 metres (3300 ft) for fear of being brought down by flying debris.

'But I continue to exert all my strength on the stick. I am aware of nothing outside the cockpit. A black film descends over my eyes and I lose consciousness for a moment. I have still not fully recovered my senses when I hear my gunner shouting "She's blown up!"

'I look out to discover that we are tearing along at full speed only a few metres above the surface of the water. I risk a gentle bank. There, over my shoulder, I see the *Marat* with a huge column of smoke towering a good 3500 metres (11,000 ft) above her. Obviously her magazines have exploded!'

Rudel's bomb had, in fact, blown the entire bow section – including 'A' turret – off the *Marat*. But the elderly battleship settled on an even keel in the shallow waters of Kronstadt harbour and the Soviets managed to get its three other main turrets back into commission. The vessel's remaining nine 12-inch guns then continued to bombard the German forces laying siege to Leningrad.

Oberleutnant Rudel had got back to Tyrkovo in one piece, courtesy of a Bf 109 from JG 54 which shot a Russian *Rata* off his tail during the return flight. But after Hauptmann Steen touched down back at base, he inadvertently ran one wheel of his machine into a bomb crater, damaging its propeller. Thus, when the order was given for a second mission to be flown – this time targeting the cruiser *Kirov* – he had to take a replacement aircraft, only to damage this one as he taxied out to take-off. With the rest of the *Gruppe* gunning their machines and ready to roll, the *Kommandeur* had no other option but to dash across to Rudel's machine, which he hastily commandeered, complete with resident back seat gunner. The attack on the *Marat* had been Steen's 300th mission of the war to date. He was fated not to return from his 301st.

In the middle of his dive on the *Kirov*, when at about 1600 metres (5250 ft), a well-placed burst of flak shredded the tail control surfaces of Steen's borrowed mount. Witnesses reported seeing him trying to aim the stricken machine at the cruiser by use of the ailerons alone, but he was unsuccessful. The Stuka and its occupants crashed into the water close alongside the vessel, which was badly damaged by the bomb Steen had released only moments earlier.

On 17 October Hauptmann Ernst-Siegfried Steen became the first eastern front Stuka pilot to be honoured with a posthumous Knight's Cross. By that date, however, a further eight Knight's Crosses had been awarded (see Appendix 2 for details), and as two of these decorations had been conferred upon members of IV.(Stuka)/LG 1, now is perhaps an opportune moment briefly to chronicle the activities of the eighth *Stukagruppe* to be involved in the war against the Soviet Union.

As its designation indicates, IV.(St)/LG 1 began life as part of the Luftwaffe's first *Lehrgeschwader*. This unit was established in the years before the war, its purpose being to evaluate the new aircraft then being produced for the Luftwaffe and to determine the best methods of employing them operationally. Each of the *Geschwader's* five component *Gruppen* was responsible for one particular class of aircraft, and IV. *Gruppe's* remit was the dive-bomber, or Stuka.

. . . and the towering column of smoke rising from the battleship after Oberleutnant Rudel's 1000-kg bomb had blown off her bows

A Ju 87R-2 of IV.(St)/LG 1 'somewhere in the north'. Despite the muddy conditions, the fresh timber lying around and the construction work going on in the background right suggests that this is to be the site of a new airstrip

By the outbreak of war, however, IV.(St)/LG 1 was serving as a regular frontline unit, seeing action both in Poland and during the *Blitzkrieg* in the west. And when Operation *Barbarossa* was launched on 22 June 1941, IV.(St)/LG 1 was the sole *Stukagruppe* assigned to *Luftflotte* 5 in the far north above the Arctic Circle. Under the command of Hauptmann Bernd von Brauchitsch, the unit's 36 Junkers Ju 87s were based at Kirkenes in northern Norway, separated from the Russian border by a narrow strip of Finnish territory, and only some 100 miles (160 km) away from the port of Murmansk.

The original intention had apparently been to employ IV.(St)/LG 1's long-range Ju 87Rs against Soviet shipping out in the Barents Sea, but in the event they were used instead primarily in a tactical role – supporting the limited movements of German ground forces in the far north, as well as to attack the port of Murmansk itself and the strategically vital railway supply line running from it down into central Russia.

But the first priority, as on the main sectors to the south, had been the neutralisation of the enemy's air force. Bad weather and thick fog prevented operations on 22 June, however, and it was not until the fourth day of the campaign that von Brauchitsch's Stukas took part in strikes on Soviet fighter bases around Murmansk, where, incredibly, they caught the enemy aircraft on the ground 'still parked wingtip to wingtip'. For the next few days the Stukas supported the early stages of XIX. Mountain Corps' advance, through Finland, across the frontier towards Murmansk.

Then on 1 July (the day veteran dive-bomber pilot Hauptmann Arnulf Blasig replaced Bernd von Brauchitsch as *Kommandeur*) the *Gruppe* was rushed 250 miles (400 km) southwards to Rovaniemi, in Finland. Here, astride the Arctic Circle, a drive by XXXVI. Army Corps across the Finnish-Soviet border that was aimed at cutting the Murmansk-Moscow rail link was meeting unexpectedly strong enemy resistance. Blasig's Stukas flew four or five missions a day – each a round trip of 200+ miles (320 km) from Rovaniemi to the fighting front at Salla and back – for almost a week before the Russian defences were finally broken.

But air operations on and above the Arctic Circle were a microcosm of the Luftwaffe's fortunes in the east as a whole. There simply were not the numbers to carry out all the tasks required of it. And although two of Blasig's *Staffeln* returned to Kirkenes as soon as the situation around Salla had been stabilised, the mountain troops' advance on Murmansk had, in the meantime, ground almost to a halt for want of effective air support. The Russian port would be heavily bombed in the weeks and months ahead, but it would not be captured. And through it – once the western allies' Arctic convoys began to operate – would flow an ever increasing stream of British and American war material for onward transport by rail down into the heart of the USSR.

CHAPTER ONE

Just how quickly, IV.(St)/LG 1 had become thinly-stretched is graphically illustrated by its commitments during one 24-hour period in mid-July – less than a month after the launch of *Barbarossa*. Fifteen aircraft were sent to bomb a railway station on the Salla front, nine despatched to attack artillery emplacements on the Rybachiy Peninsula bypassed by the advancing XIX. Mountain Corps, another nine to mount a raid on Murmansk and seven ordered to destroy an important river bridge. And although the latter was hit, it was back in use again five hours later!

This division of its responsibilities – called upon to answer urgent appeals for help from embattled ground units on the one hand, while at the same time trying to disrupt the stream of western supplies through Murmansk on the other – was to add greatly to the *Gruppe's* difficulties. Both tasks were equally vital, yet neither could be carried to a successful conclusion. In the Arctic, there were none of the spectacular ground advances and huge cauldron battles such as those that gave the Stuka units on the main sectors of the front to the south full rein to demonstrate their capabilities as 'flying artillery'. And although bombing attacks reportedly severed the Murmansk railway line more than a hundred times in the first six months of the war in the north, the tracks were always rapidly repaired again and it was never out of action for long.

IV.(St)/LG 1's missions were proving costly too. In those same six months the *Gruppe* lost 22 of its original complement of 36 aircraft. Despite everything, however, operations continued to be flown for as long as the weather held.

On 4 September *Gruppenkommandeur* Hauptmann Arnulf Blasig became the first member of IV.(St)/LG 1 to be awarded the Knight's Cross. Five weeks later, on 10 October, Oberleutnant Johannes Pfeiffer, the *Kapitän* of his 12. *Staffel*, was similarly decorated. But it was also on this latter date that Hitler finally abandoned his plans to capture Murmansk and ordered his armies in the north onto the defensive instead. This edict effectively sentenced the mountain troops fighting in the Arctic to years of trench warfare. In fact, replace the icy tundra with Flanders mud, and the far northern Russian campaign was perhaps the closest World War 2 came to replicating the miseries and horrors of the western front of 1914-18.

Not all of IV.(St)/LG 1's losses were the result of enemy action. Despite having the forward sections of its wheel-spats removed (or torn off?), this machine has been unable to cope with the soft ground and has somersaulted on landing

A light dusting of snow indicates that temperatures are falling and firming up the rutted surfaces of this dispersal point as an aircraft of 11. *Staffel* is refuelled from a bowser in preparation for its next mission. Note the unusual heads – possibly protective covers – on the *Dinortstäbe* of the underwing bombs

As winter proper sets in, bomb loads are simply tipped off the back of a truck into the deep snow surrounding each dispersal

In the sunny south the pilot of this fully loaded 'Berta' of 4./StG 77 – note the 'cockerel' badge just visible below the windscreen quarter-light – guns his engine prior to take-off

But while the ground troops were starting to dig themselves in, the Stukas of IV.(St)/LG 1 maintained the offensive for a few weeks longer. Having moved forward to captured Soviet airfields to the southeast of Salla, they were now able to attack the Murmansk railway around Kandalaksha and along the shores of the White Sea without the need for the long-range underwing fuel tanks that had been required for the long haul to the target areas from Rovaniemi. However, as October drew to a close, heavy snowfalls and the ever-shorter hours of Arctic daylight brought even these missions slowly but surely to a standstill.

Meanwhile, far removed from the barren, icy Barents and White Sea regions, the three *Gruppen* of StG 77 had spent the late summer and early autumn weeks in support of the German and Rumanian forces pushing eastwards through the Ukraine and along the Black Sea coast.

The main focus in the early stages of the campaign in the Ukraine had been the capture of the capital, Kiev. The city fell to 6. *Armee* on 19 September. But while II. and III./StG 77 had been covering the army's drive on Kiev, I./StG 77 under Hauptmann Helmut Bruck – who was to be awarded the Knight's Cross on 4 September – had been operating along the Black Sea coastal belt. The enemy was not giving up his naval bases easily, and StG 77's Stukas flew numerous overwater missions during this period against units of the Soviet Black Sea Fleet that were either escorting convoys carrying reinforcements, bombarding the advancing Axis ground forces or covering attempts at amphibious landings behind the frontlines.

On 18 August, for example, elements of StG 77 caught the Soviet submarine *D-6* some 60 miles (96 km) west of Sevastopol. And less than three weeks later, on 7 September, they bombed the destroyer *Sposobny* in Odessa harbour. Although neither vessel was sunk in these actions, both were now living on borrowed time. *D-6* managed to limp back to

During the late summer and early autumn of 1941 the Ju 87s of StG 77 were on occasion escorted by fighters of the CSIR (Italian Expeditionary Corps in Russia). Here, a Macchi MC.200 of 371° *Squadriglia* tucks in close alongside the *Staffelkapitän* of 4./StG 77

An armourer reloads the port 7.9 mm MG 17 wing machine gun of this aircraft of the *Stabskette* II./StG 77

Sevastopol, where aircraft of the *Geschwader* destroyed it while still undergoing repair in drydock on 12 November. The *Sposobny* was to be granted a somewhat longer reprieve. A further two years would pass before StG 77 finally sent the vessel to the bottom of the Black Sea.

Several strikes were then mounted against the 8000-ton Soviet cruiser *Krasny Kavkaz* which was shelling Rumanian positions in front of Odessa on 12 September. No hits were scored, but StG 77 machines did manage to sink the monitor *Udarniy* southeast of the port exactly one week later.

As already noted, 19 September was also the day that Kiev fell. And during the week that followed, the area to the east of the Ukrainian capital was to be the scene of one of the largest 'cauldron' battles of the entire war. By the time it ended on 26 September, two-thirds of a million Russian troops had been taken prisoner and the fighting strength of the entire Soviet Southwest Front had been effectively shattered. Naval operations in the Black Sea continued unabated, however, and it was here that StG 77 was next called upon to intervene in strength.

On 21 September a 2000-strong Soviet marine assault force sailed from the Crimea. Its objective was to break the Rumanian stranglehold around Odessa. En route, one of the force's four escorting destroyers, the *Frunze*, was detached to assist the gunboat *Krasnaya Armeniya* which was under attack by StG 77 off Tendra Island. The Stukas promptly sank both ships, together with the naval harbour tug *OP-8*, which had also been sent out to help.

The Soviet landings took place east of Odessa during the night of 21/22 September as planned. Early next morning, StG 77 was again in action. Finding the three remaining destroyers still in the area bombarding Rumanian positions on shore, the Stukas damaged the *Bezuprechny* with a series of near misses and scored at least one direct hit on the bows of its sister ship *Bezposhchadny*. The latter was towed stern-first to temporary safety in Odessa, but both ships would subsequently succumb to air attack, the *Bezuprechny* sunk by Ju 88s off Yalta in mid-1942, and the *Bezposhchadny* falling victim to StG 77 in the same attack that was to claim the *Sposobny* off the Crimea on 6 October 1943.

StG 77 was not engaged exclusively against shipping. After bypassing Odessa (which the Soviets would evacuate by sea during the first half of October), Axis ground forces had reached the Perekop Isthmus – the narrow tongue of land leading down on to the Crimean Peninsula – by mid-September. But the isthmus was defended in great depth, and it would take more than a month for the German 11. *Armee* to break through and gain a foothold on the Crimea itself. During this time the ground forces were supported by the dive-bombers of StG 77, who also covered the continuing drive eastwards by 1. *Panzerarmee* along the northern shores of the Sea of Azov towards Rostov-on-Don.

After damaging the destroyer *Bodry* on 31 October, StG 77's last major naval prize of the year was the 7000-ton cruiser *Chervonaya Ukraina*, which was part of a small force shelling German troops attacking the fortress harbour of Sevastopol on the south-western tip of the Crimea on 12 November. The elderly cruiser took three direct hits and, despite desperate attempts to keep her afloat, slowly filled with water and sank in shallow water. Some of her guns were subsequently removed and used ashore to augment Sevastopol's already formidable defences. The hulk was finally destroyed in a bombing attack in the spring of 1942.

On land things were not going so smoothly. 1. *Panzerarmee* had captured Rostov-on-Don on 2 November, but unexpectedly strong counter-attacks by the Red Army had wrested the city back from the Germans before the month was out. It was the first major reversal suffered by the Wehrmacht in Russia. And StG 77 was among the Luftwaffe units rushed to the area to prevent the loss of Rostov from developing into an even greater crisis.

The important role played by the *Geschwader* on the southern sector during the last quarter of 1941 – not only in supporting ground forces, but also in combating the activities of the Soviet Black Sea Fleet – was recognised by the conferral of Knight's Crosses on its two other *Gruppenkommandeure*. After Helmut Bruck's award on 4 September, both Hauptleute Helmuth Bode of III./StG 77 and II. *Gruppe's* Alfons 'Ali' Orthofer were similarly honoured on 10 October and 23 November respectively. On the latter date, a Knight's Cross also went to Oberleutnant Hermann Ruppert, *Kapitän* of 6./StG 77, whose *Staffel* had alone been credited with sinking five of the ten Soviet warships claimed by II. *Gruppe* in the Black Sea to date, as well as four merchantmen.

But individual, even unit, prowess was no match for that one implacable foe of any foreign invader daring to set foot on Russian soil – 'General Winter'. Although conditions in the south of the country were by no means as harsh as those being suffered by IV.(St)/LG 1 in the Arctic, they were severe enough to restrict operations to a minimum – which did, in turn, at least enable most crews to be withdrawn from the frontline for a brief period of rest and relaxation.

And what of events on the central sector since the late summer? Operation *Barbarossa* had originally been planned and launched with one major aim in view – to capture the Soviet capital, Moscow. That objective remained, but after StGs 2 and 77 had, of necessity, been transferred away to the Baltic and Black Sea areas, the Stukas remaining to *Luftflotte* on the Central front – comprising just II. and III,/StG 1, with less than 50 serviceable Ju 87s in all – were hopelessly inadequate for the task in hand.

While Army Group Centre continued its main thrust towards the capital along the axis of the Minsk-Moscow highway, extracts from the logbook of Major Walter Hagen, *Kommodore* of StG 1, reveal that the *Geschwader* spent much of August over 100 miles (160 km) to the north of the highway, where the Red Army was resisting stubbornly around the town of Velikiye Luki. Here, there were no shipping targets – except perhaps for the odd river barge or gunboat – and StG 1 concentrated its operations on ground support, as these unit diary entries detail;

11 August – Attack road bridge at Frol
12 August, 0530 hrs – Attack railway at Velikiye Luki, with direct hit on train

Hauptmann Helmut Bruck, *Kommandeur* of I./StG 77 (left), confers with his *Geschwaderkommodore*, a well wrapped-up Oberst Clemens *Graf* von Schönborn-Wiesentheid, in Kharkov during the winter of 1941-42

12 August, 1725 hrs – Attack railway at Velikiye Luki, cutting track in four places

23 August – Target troops southeast of Velikiye Luki, causing *wild chaos* among enemy ground troops

29 August – Target troops around Lake Duringe , with direct hits on earthworks and fortifications.

It was not only the Red Army that was now beginning to offer a more organised defence. In the air, the Luftwaffe was meeting stiffer resistance from its Soviet counterparts. By the end of August a total of 146 Stukas had been lost in Russia, and a further 49 damaged. One of the last casualties during this period was Hauptmann Anton Keil, the long-serving *Gruppenkommandeur* of II./StG 1, who had won his Knight's Cross at the height of the Battle of Britain. On 29 August, during the course of yet another strike against the enemy's rail network in the Velikiye Luki area, Keil was forced to make an emergency landing behind Russian lines. But like so much of this region, the stretch of open ground he selected was, in fact, a swamp. The Stuka somersaulted and both Hauptmann Keil and his gunner were killed in the crash.

Having lost one Knight's Cross wearer, the *Geschwader* promptly gained another just 24 hours later when Oberleutnant Hartmut Schairer, the *Staffelkapitän* of 7./StG 1, received the award on 30 August.

Early in September Major Hagen's Stukas transferred from Surash to Sezhchinskaya, some 90 miles (145 km) south-southeast of Smolensk. Their role remained one primarily of ground support. This new area of operations to the south of the Moscow highway was to be the jumping-off point for the right-hand flank of the forthcoming final assault on the Soviet capital. But here too enemy resistance had hardened.

In the first half of the month StG 1's pilots flew numerous missions against Red Army units trying to dislodge German troops from the Yelnya salient. And it was one of their number – a young Leutnant of III./StG 1 who was already making something of a name for himself for attacking and knocking-out Soviet anti-aircraft emplacements – who would receive the *Stukawaffe's* next eastern front Knight's Cross. The decoration awarded to 'Theo' Nordmann on 17 September was to be the first of many honours. He would be the *Kommodore* of a *Schlachtgeschwader* and wearing the Swords by the time he was killed in his Fw 190 early in 1945.

By the end of September, preparations for Operation *Taifun* (Typhoon), the all-out offensive aimed at capturing Moscow, were complete. The bulk of VIII. *Fliegerkorps*, including the Stukas of StG 2, had been brought back down from the Leningrad front to support *Panzergruppe* 3's left-hook to the north of the Soviet capital. To the south, elements of StG 77 were sent up from the Ukraine to add their weight to StG 1's two *Gruppen*.

An ageing Ju 87B-1 still doing her bit in the late summer of 1941 thanks to some 'TLC' from a crowd of black-overalled ground mechanics. While most seem to have completed their tasks, the man on the wing root gives a final check to the oil

A *'Berta'* of II./StG 1 labours for height. Although the ventral bomb release yoke swings empty, all four 50-kg (110 lb) underwing bombs – complete with percussion fuse rods and tail screamers – are still *in situ*

Launched on 2 October, *Taifun* began with a textbook double-pincer movement. Supported by *Luftflotte* 2's Ju 87s, three *Panzergruppen* – from north to south, 3, 4 and 2 respectively – broke through the Soviet front along a 300-mile (480 km) stretch straddling the Moscow highway. Deep in the enemy's rear, the armoured spearheads then joined forces, trapping huge numbers of Red Army troops in pockets around the towns of Vyazma and Bryansk.

The largest of these pockets was that to the west of Vyazma, a town situated on the highway less than 150 miles (240 km) from the Soviet capital. Here, *Panzergruppen* 3 and 4 had encircled the six armies of Marshal Timoshenko's West Front. The two smaller pockets either side of Bryansk some way to the south held another three armies of Marshal Yeremenko's aptly named Bryansk Front. The twin battles of Vyazma and Bryansk, fought during the first two weeks of October, reduced all three pockets. The last armies in the field in front of Moscow's own outer defence ring had been eliminated. The way to the capital was open, and it was ready for the taking.

Hitler had not waited even this long to trumpet the end of the Soviet Union. On only the second day of *Taifun* he had announced that the enemy was 'already broken and would never rise again'. And four days after that he decreed that no capitulation of Moscow was to be accepted. He wanted to raze Stalin's capital to the ground. The following week the Reich's press chief, Dr Otto Dietrich, was still echoing the official line. 'The military decision in the east has been settled and Russia is done for!'

However, those doing the actual fighting were not so sure. Even before the Vyazma-Bryansk pockets had been completely eliminated, Moscow itself was facing the very real danger of attack from two sides, with 3. *Panzerarmee* (the *Panzergruppen* had been elevated to army status in the opening stages of *Taifun*) striking towards Kalinin to the north of the capital and 2. *Panzerarmee* driving up towards Tula from the south.

But on 13 October, the day Kalinin was taken, came the first reports of snow and sleet showers on the central sector. Forty-eight hours later nearly eight inches (20 cm) of loose snow fell, making take-offs difficult. 'General Winter' was beginning to show his hand, and the portents were not good. Stuka units were still being called to the aid of ground troops despite the increasingly adverse conditions. Having moved forward from Staritsa to newly-occupied Kalinin, I./StG 2 was instrumental on 21 October in breaking up a Soviet counter-attack that had surrounded and cut off a large part of 1. *Panzerdivision* close to the town.

A week later the Red Army got closer still, subjecting Kalinin airfield to heavy artillery bombardment. Once again I./StG 2 helped to avert the danger. While the Stukas went out hunting for the enemy gun positions hidden in the nearby woods, members of the *Gruppe's* groundcrews took up arms to defend the field itself from infantry attack.

CHAPTER ONE

By the end of October the daily advances made by *Taifun*, which had kicked off so spectacularly, were being measured in mere yards. The early snow showers were now interspersed by long hours of constant, heavy, icy rain. It was the start of the so-called mud period. As one senior Luftwaffe officer noted in his diary;

'Our bold hopes have disappeared under rain and snow. Everything is at a standstill on the bottomless roads, and while the temperatures continue to drop, we get 10 to 15 centimetres (four to six inches) of snow followed by yet more rain.'

The term 'bottomless mud' occurs time and again in diaries and accounts of this period. And while this may be an exaggeration, most roads and tracks were indeed transformed into runnels of viscous, cloying mud three feet (90 cm) deep or more. The only things that could move were tracked vehicles and *panje* carts – and even these only with greatest difficulty. Yet still the pilots of StGs 1, 2 and 77 continued to support the armoured units inching their way towards Moscow.

Russia's 'mud period' is usually of fairly short duration, and the late autumn of 1941 was no exception. But it was followed by something far worse for the invading German forces. Early in November, temperatures began to fall further still and surfaces hardened. Ground movement was possible again, but only briefly. On 6 November, units of XXIII. *Armeekorps*, supported by the Stukas of StG 2, managed to advance nine miles (15 km) closer to Moscow. But 24 hours later there were yet more heavy snowfalls and the thermometer dropped to 20 degrees below zero. And it would continue not simply to drop, but to plummet. The great freeze had begun.

Hitler had not intended to wage a long war in the east. He had envisioned a brief *Blitzkrieg* campaign against an unprepared Soviet Union. But his plans had been thrown awry, and the launch of *Barbarossa*

Russia's 'mud period'. A Kfz. 11 Wanderer staff car of I./StG 77 throws up a bow wave as it negotiates a flooded, but still passable, roadway bordering a forward landing ground. In the distance, a *Gruppe* aircraft is almost marooned by the rising water

A *panje* pony drawing a sledge plods past in the background completely unconcerned by the noise and powdered snow being kicked up by this taxiing Stuka

delayed, by events in the Balkans in the spring of 1941. Now his armies in the field were paying the price. Troops and groundcrews had neither winter clothing nor suitable accommodation. Weapons and vehicles lacked special lubricants and heating equipment. The former problem was partially addressed by appeals for donations of warm clothing, particularly women's fur coats, from the civil population back in Germany. But the mechanical difficulties were well nigh insuperable.

And still the Stukas responded to pleas for help from their comrades on the ground. Desperate measures were needed. With temperatures dropping to 40 below, engines refused to start. Open fires had to be lit on the ground beneath them to thin the oil and prewarm their moving parts. Fog and heavy snow then kept the *Staffeln* grounded for days on end. But given the slightest chance the crews would take off, even if the cloud base was as low as 150 ft (45 m) and visibility down to 1000 yards (900 m).

As November drew to a close, however, operational activity inevitably began to decline. On 13 November aircraft of StG 2 beat off a Soviet attack on their own field at Rusa, some 55 miles (90 km) west of Moscow, to which they had transferred after being forced to evacuate Kalinin. Five days later they broke up a large concentration of enemy troops preparing for another assault.

On 26 November StG 1's *Staffeln* flew a number of sorties in support of 2. *Panzerarmee* which was still trying, unsuccessfully, to take Tula from the south. And 28 November proved to be a day of such rare good weather that it enabled all Stuka units on the central sector to fly as many as four missions each as 2. *Panzerarmee's* leading divisions made one final attempt, again without success, to dislodge the Red Army from its positions around Tula.

As a gaggle of nine Stukas barely visible in the background peel off to come in for a landing, 9./StG 1's 'J9+LL' undergoes some essential engine maintenance out in the open (note the mechanic's legs atop the cowling in front of the windscreen). A close-up shot of the nose of this same machine shows that it bore the name *Moshaisk* (Mozhaysk), presumably to commemorate its participation in the recent fighting for the town of that name some 60 miles (96 km) west of Moscow

As winter tightened its grip, open air maintenance became ever more difficult. Lucky were the units that had the use of heated tents such as that shown here. Luftwaffe mechanics called these canvas structures *'Kaffeewärmer'* (literally 'coffee-warmers'), but the nearest English equivalent would perhaps be 'tea-cosies'!

CHAPTER ONE

And, if all else failed, the last resort for coaxing a frozen engine back into life was to light a fire underneath it, which is exactly what is going on here. Mechanics of 4./StG 77 have placed a pile of logs directly beneath the radiator intake of this B-2, and they are about to put a match to them, while others try to persuade that recalcitrant propeller to turn

The original German caption to this photograph describes it as a 'Stuka attack on a Soviet HQ in the fortified citadel, or kremlin, of Teryayevo, 35 kilometres (22 miles) northwest of Moscow'. Although the buildings appear to be undamaged, smoke is rising from a bomb hit on, or near, the outer defensive wall

On the last day of the month it was 4. *Panzerarmee*, still clawing its way along the line of the Moscow highway, that was to enjoy the benefit of Stuka support. This army came closest to attaining the great prize. A reconnaissance troop from one of its forward units, *Panzerpionierbataillon* 62, managed to advance over eight miles (12 km) and reached the village of Khimki, less than five miles (8 km) from the outskirts of the Soviet capital. The invaders were now little more than a tram ride away from the walls of the Kremlin! They would get no further.

At the beginning of December the German offensive finally froze to a halt in temperatures that had sunk to as low as minus 50 degrees. With his hopes for a speedy conquest of the USSR dashed, the *Führer* promptly ordered the bulk of *Luftflotte* 2 – the air fleet assigned to the central sector of the eastern front – to be transferred to the Mediterranean theatre. And on 8 December he issued War Directive No 39 decreeing how the war against Russia was to be conducted during the winter months ahead;

'The severe winter weather which has come unexpectedly early in the east, and the consequent difficulties in bringing up supplies, compel us to abandon immediately all major offensive operations and to go over to the defensive. The task of the Luftwaffe is to prevent the rehabilitation of the Russian forces by attacking, as far as possible, equipment and training centres. As well as engaging the enemy air force, the Luftwaffe will support the army by all available means in defence against enemy attacks on the ground and in the air. I reserve to myself the right to authorise the withdrawal from the Moscow front of those forces still allocated for service with Commander-in-Chief South (Mediterranean).'

Hitler's order to go on the defensive did not come in time to save Oberleutnant Joachim Rieger, the long-serving *Staffelkapitän* of 5./StG 1, whose machine had been accidentally rammed by his wingman when their formation came under attack from Soviet fighters close to Moscow on 2 December. 'Bulle' Rieger would be honoured with a posthumous Knight's Cross on 19 March 1942.

The last sentence of the *Führer's* war directive quoted above clearly referred to VIII. *Fliegerkorps* – the only part of *Luftflotte* 2 not to have departed for the Mediterranean. In the event, Hitler did not exercise his 'right' to send it to join the rest of the air fleet in sunnier climes. Instead it was to remain on the Moscow front where it took on the role of 'air fleet-in-being', shouldering sole responsibility for the entire central sector.

The corps' Stukas thus represented the only strike force in front of Moscow during the winter of 1941-42. Or, rather, some of them did, for such was the dearth of Luftwaffe activity during this period that nearly half of the *Stukagruppen* deployed in the east were withdrawn from the front early in December 1941 for rest and re-equipment. III./StG 1 and I./StG 2

Little sign of recent, or imminent, aerial activity here as an unidentified 'Berta' squats out in the open, uppersurfaces covered in a thick mantle of snow and makeshift rudder lock firmly in place. Even the Ju 52/3m in the background – the untiring 'workhorse' of the Luftwaffe – seems to be in hibernation, its cockpit and dorsal gun position shrouded against the elements

Keeping up the pressure on the southern sector. Just back from a mission, a machine of the *Gruppenstab* I./StG 77 taxies in to its dispersal, where armourers are already waiting with a fresh load of bombs

were both sent back to the homeland – to Schweinfurt and Böblingen, respectively – while II./StG 77, which had been seconded to VIII. *Fliegerkorps* for *Taifun*, retired to Cracow, in Poland.

This meant that, excluding IV.(St)/LG 1 in the Arctic, there were just four *Stukagruppen* in the whole of Russia as 1941 drew to a close. To the south, in the Ukraine, on the Crimea and over the Black Sea, where the temperatures were not quite so extreme (only minus 10 in places!), I. and III./StG 77 were keeping up the pressure on the Red Army and Navy. But on the central sector the Stukas pulled back to well defended bases, II./StG 1 to Sezhchinskaya, northwest of Bryansk, and III./StG 2 to Dugino, north of Vyazma, where they dug in for winter.

During the last quarter of 1941 another six Knight's Crosses had been awarded, all to members of StG 2 (see Appendix 2). But individual decorations could not disguise the fact that the year had ended in failure in the east. And when operations began again in earnest in the spring of 1942, they would herald the beginning of the end of the Stuka's dive-bombing career on the Russian front. The machine – in the refined shape of the new and improved Ju 87D variants – was still to see more than 18 months of frontline service, however.

But during that time opposition from a revived Red Air Force would grow steadily stronger and the Stuka's inherent weaknesses – limited speed and manoeuvrability, and inadequate defensive firepower, which the modifications to the D-model had addressed, but not eliminated – would gradually begin to tell upon it. It may have been faint, but the writing was already on the wall.

CHAPTER TWO

1942 – ROAD TO ARMAGEDDON

Having been forced to withdraw from their forwardmost bases, German ground and air units on the Moscow front spent the opening weeks of 1942 fighting off a succession of heavy counter-attacks by fresh Siberian divisions brought in by Stalin to defend his capital city.

The first three Stuka Knight's Crosses of the New Year were all awarded on 6 January. One of them went to Oberleutnant Hans-Ulrich Rudel of I./StG 2. His outstanding achievement to date had undoubtedly been the crippling of the battleship *Marat*. But the citation went on to make mention of some of his other successes since, including the destruction or damaging of 15 bridges, 23 artillery emplacements, four armoured trains and 17 tanks and self-propelled guns.

The misfit Rudel – dubbed by one of his pre-war superiors 'a very odd fish indeed' – was finally becoming accepted, although apparently not yet by all. For it was Oberleutnant Rudel who was subsequently selected to be taken off operations and returned to Austria as *Kapitän* of StG 2's *Ergänzungsstaffel*, the unit charged with preparing newly trained crews for frontline service with the *Geschwader*.

Also back in the Reich at the beginning of 1942 an entirely new II./StG 2 was being formed. The original II./StG 2, which had first seen the light of day as I./StG 162 in 1938, had flown as a semi-autonomous *Gruppe* in both the Polish and French campaigns, before operating as part of StG 3 during the Battle of Britain and in the Mediterranean. At the height of the campaign in North Africa, on 13 January 1942, it was officially incorporated into the latter *Geschwader* by being designated III./StG 3. And it was to fill the now vacant II. *Gruppe* slot in StG 2 that the new unit had been set up at Neukuhren, in East Prussia. Led by Hauptmann Dr Ernst Kupfer, it was created around intakes from both I./StG 2 (currently back in the Reich converting onto the Ju 87D) and the *Ergänzungsstaffel*.

When a new II./StG 2 was activated in January 1942 for service on the eastern front, its appointed *Gruppenkommandeur*, Hauptmann Dr Ernst Kupfer, selected as the unit badge the 'Horseman of Bamberg' in tribute to his home town

Caught on an open road, a Soviet tank 'brews up' after taking a direct hit – a perfect example of the Stuka's fabled pin-point accuracy

With no Stukas at all in the northern sector, and with both II./StG 1 and III./StG 2 hard pressed on the Moscow front, the only offensive dive-bomber activity in the east early in 1942 was that being carried out by I. and III./StG 77 in the southern sector. On 4 January, for example, six machines of StG 77 caught the Soviet cruiser *Krasny Kavkaz* off the Crimean coast – this was the vessel the *Geschwader's* pilots had attacked the previous September while it was shelling Axis troops outside Odessa. They had scored no hits on that occasion. Nor did they this time when they found the cruiser retiring at high speed after a similar action bombarding German forces now besieging Sevastopol. But four near misses close to her stern damaged the *Krasny Kavkaz* so severely that she was out of action for the next ten months.

It was in support of the ground troops of Army Group South that StG 77's Stukas were, however, most active. In the closing weeks of 1941 they had already been instrumental in breaking up a Soviet counter-offensive west of Rostov after that city had been recaptured by the Red Army. They continued to assist in the defence of the River Mius line north of Taganrog into the new year, but then the focus of operations switched from the Ukraine back down on to the Crimea.

11. *Armee* had finally battered its way through the defences of the Perekop Isthmus – the narrow neck of land leading down to the Crimea – after more than a month of heavy fighting the previous autumn. But it had still not yet cleared the peninsula entirely of the enemy. Although completely surrounded, the fortress harbour of Sevastopol on the southwest tip of the Crimea was holding out. Even more serious, perhaps, Soviet forces had re-crossed the Kerch Straits separating the Crimea from the Caucasus and landed behind German lines. By the first week of January the eastern part of the peninsula was back in Russian hands.

During the night of 4/5 January the Soviets mounted an even more audacious landing, putting a battalion of marines ashore at Yevpatoria – a port on the western side of the Crimea. The *Krasny Kavkaz* had been shelling German positions around Sevastopol, less than 50 miles (80 km) down the coast, in a bid to draw attention away from this amphibious assault. The Yevpatoria landing was a step too far, and the Germans reacted furiously. Relentless dive-bombing by the Stukas of StG 77 forced the surviving Soviet marines into surrender within a week. But that still left the problem of Kerch at the eastern end of the peninsula.

It was to be the Luftwaffe's job to redress the situation. On the personal orders of *Reichsmarschall* Göring, a *Sonderstab Krim* (Special Staff Crimea) was established specifically for the purpose. Commencing operations in mid-January, the *Sonderstab's* three *Kampfgruppen* were used to attack the Soviet's Black Sea ports and ships at sea supplying the Kerch landings, while StG 77's Stukas were tasked with the close support of the ground troops attempting to push the enemy back across the Kerch Straits. III./StG 77 was now paired with II. *Gruppe*, recently returned to the front after its brief period of rest and refit (and thereby releasing I./StG 77 as the next unit for transfer back to Germany and re-equipment with the Ju 87D).

But within a month Göring was forced to order the disbandment of the *Sonderstab Krim*. A renewed Red Army offensive had smashed its way across the River Donetz at Izyum some 281 miles (450 km) to the north of the Crimea. This posed a far greater threat than the enemy troops penned in at Kerch, and the bulk of the *Sonderstab*'s bombers were urgently needed on the mainland southern sector. Among those sent up into the Ukraine were the Stukas of II./StG 77.

III. *Gruppe*, meanwhile, continued to pound away at Kerch. On 24 February some two-dozen of its machines attacked and destroyed enemy artillery positions covering the Parpach Line – the front that the Soviet defenders of Kerch had established across the 11-mile (18 km) neck of land that separated them from the main body of the Crimea. Five days later, after an intervening spell of bad weather, III./StG 77 mounted 40 individual sorties, claiming nearly 20 Red Army tanks damaged or destroyed near the northern end of the Parpach Line. On 2 and 3 March it returned to the same area, inflicting further damage to enemy armour and transport.

On the Donetz front II./StG 77 was finding the going tougher. The *Gruppe* suffered a number of losses, including the *Kapitän* of 6. *Staffel*, Oberleutnant Hermann Ruppert, whose machine was shot down in flames by Soviet fighters south of Izyum on 2 March.

The final all-out assault to clear the Kerch bridgehead would not be launched for another eight weeks, by which time I./StG 77 had returned from Germany with its new *Doras* and was based, together with the other elements of the *Geschwader*, on the complex of airfields around Sarabuz, near the centre of the Crimea.

Operation *Trappenjagd* ('Bustard Hunt') was preceded on the afternoon of 7 May by StG 77's Stukas flying from a forward airstrip to attack Soviet anti-tank gun positions and other defences along the southern part of the Parpach Line. The ground assault went in during the early hours of the following morning. StG 77 kept up the pressure on the southern end of the enemy's defence line throughout 8 May, with most crews flying as many as five sorties during the day. Altogether, they dropped close on 200 tons of bombs.

Operations as intensive as this did not come without cost. On 9 May (a day of deteriorating weather culminating in heavy rain) II./StG 77 reported the loss of two of its aircraft. The next morning only the more experienced crews were able to take off. The fields had become quagmires overnight, and the cloud base had descended to little more than 150 ft (45 m). Operations had to be carried out at low level, leading to further casualties. And a massed

II./StG 77's new '*Doras*' did not remain pristine for long. Wheel-spats already removed, 4. *Staffel's* 'S2+NM' makes heavy going of Russia's spring mud

I./StG 77 had its problems too – a taxiing accident at Sarabuz involving two '*Doras*' of Oberleutnant Karl Henze's 1. *Staffel*

raid on 11 May, with all *Gruppen* ordered to take off at 0330 hrs, had to be aborted again because of the impossible weather conditions.

But the Luftwaffe units supporting *Trappenjagd* – and the *Stukagruppen* in particular – had done what was required of them. The demoralised enemy was already retiring towards the port of Kerch on the eastern tip of the Crimea and preparing for evacuation back across the straits to the Caucasus. The last large-scale Stuka strikes were flown on 12 May. For III./StG 77 operations were to end on a sad note 24 hours later when the machine flown by Oberleutnant Johann Waldhauser, the Knight's Cross-wearing *Kapitän* of 9. *Staffel*, took a direct flak hit while diving on a target near Kerch and never pulled out.

Kerch was finally cleared on 17 May, but by that time the Stukas of StG 77 had already left the Crimea. The Luftwaffe's dive-bomber strength in the east had never been exactly abundant, and by the early summer of 1942 the succession of Soviet counter-attacks that were being launched one after the other along the whole length of the front from the Black Sea up to the Baltic was highlighting the Stukas' lack of numbers. The Ju 87's successes to date had been derived primarily from the professionalism of one man – recently promoted Generaloberst Wolfram *Freiherr* von Richthofen, GOC VIII. *Fliegerkorps*. His consummate leadership skills had ensured that the dive-bombers under his command operated as a body to deliver carefully planned, concentrated attacks.

But this would soon no longer be possible. Events were about to force the *Stukawaffe* into the thankless role of the eastern front's 'mobile fire brigade', with *Geschwader*, *Gruppen* and even individual *Staffeln* being rushed hither and thither to the scene of the latest conflagration.

And in the second week of May the next area of the front to ignite and blaze up into furious activity was that around Kharkov. Here, the Red Army unleashed a massive counter-offensive by 39 divisions, supported by 19 tank brigades – well over a thousand armoured vehicles in all – which bypassed the city to the north and south and was soon threatening to encircle its defenders.

The first machines of StG 77 touched down at Kharkov-Rogan on the afternoon of 13 May. The remainder of the *Geschwader* arrived during the course of the next 48 hours. For the following two weeks the battlefields on either side of Kharkov were witness to a demonstration of classic Stuka warfare as the crews of StG 77 hurled themselves time and again at the hordes of Soviet tanks trying to drive a wedge through the German defences. That the enemy failed to do so was due in no small measure to the three *Gruppen* of StG 77.

Battered to a standstill, primarily by attack from the air, yet forbidden

Hauptmann Helmut Bruck, *Gruppenkommandeur* **of I./StG 77, inspects his handiwork – a Lend-Lease British Matilda tank knocked out near Kharkov on 29 May 1942**

to withdraw on the express orders of Stalin, the troops in the two Soviet salients were set upon by German forces. More than 200,000 prisoners were taken and large numbers of tanks, guns and other equipment captured. It was another catastrophic defeat for the Red Army, but it would be one of the last.

In addition to its anti-tank activities, StG 77 had also been employed against artillery positions, batteries of mobile rocket-launchers – the much-feared 'Stalin's Organs' – supply convoys and concentrations of troops. And, just in case any members of Stalin's army were rash enough to disobey his orders and try to make good their escape, the *Geschwader* brought their part in the 1942 Battle of Kharkov to a close by destroying five major bridges over the River Donetz to the rear area of the attempted breakthrough.

StG 77 had thus played a vital role in two important battles – Kerch and Kharkov – in the space of just three weeks. But the crews were not allowed to rest on their laurels. Before May was out they were rushed back down to the Crimea, where a single, but potentially highly dangerous, pocket of Soviet resistance was still holding out.

So dangerous, in fact, was the threat posed by the harbour fortress of Sevastopol to Hitler's imminent summer offensive in the southern sector that nearly the whole of VIII. *Fliegerkorps* was also diverted down to the Crimea to support the troops of 11. *Armee* in the taking of it. It would not be an easy job. The natural defences of the area, with its many ravines and gullies scoring the heights above the harbour, had been constantly added to by man – not least by the Soviets over the past two decades.

By 1942 Sevastopol was protected to landward by a 15-mile (24 km) unbroken arc of triple defences incorporating over 3500 individual fortified positions, many hacked out of solid rock, and a network of over 200 miles (320 km) of slit trenches. These were covered by a whole arsenal of weapons, ranging from machineguns to the four giant 30.5 cm guns of the *Maxim Gorky I* coastal battery housed in their armoured cupolas to the north of the harbour.

On the evening of 1 June Generaloberst von Richthofen reported that his units were in place and ready to begin the assault. StG 77's pilots were no strangers to Sevastopol. They had been attacking the harbour on and off ever since it was first surrounded back in mid-November 1941. The C-in-C of the Black Sea Fleet's naval air arm had been killed in a bombing raid by III./StG 77 as recently as 24 April. But now the air offensive against what has been described as 'the strongest fortifications in military history' was to be more systematic, for despite its massive land defences, Sevastopol was vulnerable from both air and sea. Its woefully, and inexcusably, inadequate fighter force was quickly eradicated, leaving the Luftwaffe the freedom of the skies, and it was almost completely dependent on seaborne supplies if it was to continue to hold out.

Smoke rises from Sevastopol harbour. Fort *Molotov* is visible at bottom left above the Stuka wingtip. Fort *Maxim Gorky I* is unfortunately out of shot beyond the body of water seen at top right

The GOC 11. *Armee*, Generaloberst Erich von Manstein, clearly recognised these facts, as is evident from the five-fold assistance he set down as his requirements from VIII. *Fliegerkorps*;

1. To prevent the Red Air Force from supporting the Red Army
2. Repeated day and night attacks on the fortress of Sevastopol to break the morale of the defenders
3. Direct air support of 11. *Armee's* assault units during their storming of the outer defences
4. The neutralisation of Soviet artillery by bombing, as well as observation flights to provide fire control for German counter-battery fire
5. Cutting off the Soviet troops in the fortress from supplies by sea and air

For five days prior to the actual assault, from 2 to 6 June, the defences of Sevastopol were subjected to an intense 'softening-up' bombardment from both artillery and aircraft. The former – 'the heaviest German artillery barrage ever laid down on the eastern front' – included two weapons that eclipsed even the 30.5 cm guns of fort *Maxim Gorky I*. The 60 cm tracked mortar *Karl* (more commonly known as *Thor*) had previously been employed against Brest-Litovsk in the summer of 1941. But Sevastopol was the only time the colossal 80 cm railway-gun *Dora*, originally designated to bombard the French Maginot Line, or even perhaps Gibraltar, was ever to be fired in anger.

Beginning at 0600 hrs on 2 June, StG 77's contribution to the softening-up process was a near non-stop succession of bombing raids, with crews from all three *Gruppen* flying up to as many as eight sorties a day from their bases around Sarabuz. Unless specifically ordered to head out over the coast and attack their targets from the seaward side, these missions rarely took more than 20 minutes, which hardly gave the Stukas enough time to reach their operational height before winging over into their dives. Little wonder that they were soon being referred to as 'conveyor belt' operations!

As well as pounding Sevastopol's outer ring of defences, StG 77's pilots were provided with detailed maps and aerial photographs, which allowed them to demonstrate their pinpoint accuracy in attacking specific targets. During this period they hit the town's power station, severely disrupting electricity supplies. Even worse for the defenders was the destruction of a main pumping station which cut off much of Sevastopol's water. By the end of the five days the Luftwaffe had mounted more than 3000 missions against Sevastopol, dropping 2250+ tons of bombs and close on 24,000 incendiaries on the harbour fortress and its surroundings.

Just as fighter pilots kept count of their aerial victories, so Stuka pilots assiduously recorded the number of operational missions they had flown. The 'conveyor belt' sorties carried out during the fighting for Sevastopol added considerably to many Stuka flyers' totals – including, perhaps, this unidentified pilot of 4./StG 77, later photographed on reaching his 300th. Note the unusually thick (and somewhat crooked!) *Dinortstäbe* projecting from the underwing bombs

When the ground assault troops went in at first light on 7 June, StG 77 immediately focused its attentions on the point of attack, bombing and strafing Soviet positions and the fortified villages along the northern sector of the outer defence ring. It would continue to provide direct support for the army storm units slowly battling their way through the labyrinth of forward fortifications, trenches and wire for the best part of a week while, at the same time, also responding to calls to attack such rear-area targets as heavy artillery bunkers, coastal batteries and supply shipping, both in the harbour itself and out at sea.

A sustained *Blitz* against long-range gun emplacements beginning on 14 June came to a climax three days later with the destruction of the biggest of them all. Contemporary records credit StG 77's Oberleutnant Maué with knocking out *Maxim Gorky I*. The Soviet version is that Coastal Battery 30 – its official designation – ceased firing simply because it had run out of ammunition, and was then blown up by its crews. Whatever the true facts, the silencing of this important strongpoint less than three miles (5 km) north of the harbour marked the crucial turning point of the entire battle. With the initial assault in the north about to penetrate the third and final ring of defence works, and with Rumanian and German troops pushing hard to the east and south, the Stukas were able to range further afield.

On 18 June they participated in attacks on five vessels of the Soviet Black Sea Fleet some 60 miles (95 km) off the Crimean coast. The warships were en route to Sevastopol, but near misses on the flotilla leader *Kharkov* caused such damage that she was no longer able to manoeuvre and had to be towed away by her sister-ship *Tashkent*.

With the end of the battle for Sevastopol in sight, the bulk of VIII. *Fliegerkorps* was withdrawn from the Crimea and transferred back up into the Ukraine on 23 June. Among the units remaining, StG 77 spent that day bombarding the harbour area and its innermost defences. 26 June then found its Ju 87s in action over the Black Sea again. The Soviet navy was still making desperate efforts to get supplies and reinforcements to beleaguered troops on shore. On that date the *Tashkent* managed to make it through to Sevastopol with nearly 1000 troops on board, but another destroyer was not so lucky. The *Bezuprechny*, an old adversary of the *Geschwader*, was caught by II./StG 77's Oberfeldwebel Werner Haugk and quickly sent to the bottom off Yalta. Further to the east along the coast other Stukas found and despatched the submarine *S.32*.

The following day, 27 June, fate finally caught up with the *Tashkent*. Having survived more than 40 round trips to Sevastopol, she was

An almost vertical shot taken from a Stuka – note the outline of the engine cowling at the bottom of the photograph – as it dives on coastal gun emplacements outside Sevastopol. The previous machine's bombs can be seen already bursting at the right-hand end of what appears to be a line of zigzag blast walls protecting a tank farm

Still wearing their kapok lifejackets, this 6./StG 77 crew regale a spellbound knot of ground personnel with details of their latest overwater sortie. The helmeted pilot bears more than a passing resemblance to Oberfeldwebel Werner Haugk. Could those eloquent hand gestures be describing the last moments of the Soviet destroyer *Bezuprechny* on 26 June 1942?

now subjected to a series of air attacks as she made all speed eastwards with 2300 civilians and wounded crammed aboard. Even so, it was only after four hours had passed, and nearly 350 bombs had fallen around her, that 8. *Staffel's* Oberfeldwebel Herbert Dawedait scored the near miss that put her out of action. But still she did not sink. Badly holed, and with 1900 tons of water inside her hull, she was towed to Novorossisk, where she settled on the bottom.

One final massive air and artillery bombardment on the morning of 1 July heralded the end for Sevastopol. By the early afternoon the ruined harbour was in German hands. Soviet troops held out on the Khersones Peninsula for a further week, but with the Luftwaffe now bombing the Black Sea Fleet's main bases along the Caucasus coast, there was no hope of an eleventh-hour, large-scale evacuation. The last of the 95,000 surviving defenders of Sevastopol laid down their arms and were taken into captivity.

By that time Operation *Blau* (Blue) – the 1942 summer offensive in the southern sector – was already nearly a fortnight old. But before charting the route that was to lead to the disaster of Stalingrad, it would be advisable at this juncture to catch up with those *Stukagruppen* last heard of struggling to cope with the winter conditions on the Moscow front and points north.

In the far northern Arctic theatre, IV.(St)/LG 1 emerged from a period of near hibernation to discover that the New Year would be offering very much the same as the latter half of 1941 – a division of its labour between raids on the Soviet Barents and White Sea ports and attacks on the Murmansk railway leading down into central Russia. The only differences were that the Red Air Force, as on every other sector, was becoming stronger and better organised, and that it would soon be operating under a new identity, for on 27 January 1942 IV.(St)/LG 1 was redesignated to become I./StG 5.

Despite the Soviets' establishing a chain of fighter airstrips along the Murmansk railway for the sole purpose of protecting this vital supply lifeline from air attack, I./StG 5 would continue to target it throughout the year. The Ju 87s more often than not required fighter escort of their own in order to do so successfully. And although they hit the line on numerous occasions, the Russians were always quick to repair the damage caused and – as in 1941 – it was never out of action for long.

The wearisome cycle of attacks on the Murmansk railway was a thankless and frustrating task that produced few long-term benefits and received little official or public recognition. I./StG 5's operations in support of the ground forces in the Arctic likewise resulted in little more than local appreciation from those troops in immediate receipt of their assistance. It is perhaps indicative of the mundane nature of much of I./StG 5's work in the far north during 1942-43 that none of the six Knight's Cross winners who passed through the *Gruppe's* ranks in this period actually won their award while a member of the unit.

And yet there was one area where the Stukas of I./StG 5 more than made their mark on a wider stage, and that was over the northern port of Murmansk at the height of the Allied Arctic convoy operations.

One of their earliest successes of the new year was a direct hit that severely damaged the *Lancaster Castle* during one of the two raids carried out against Murmansk on 24 March. The 5172-ton British merchantman (not to be confused with the Royal Navy's *Castle*-class corvette of the same name that participated in some of the last Arctic convoys of the war) had been part of convoy PQ 12 which had arrived in Russia on 12 March. Anchored in the roads off Murmansk, the damaged vessel was finally sunk in another bombing raid on 14 April. Nine days later the *Gruppe* sent two of the port's resident smaller fry to the bottom – the harbour tugboat *Stroitel* and a 45-ton floating crane. On a second mission on that same 23 April, seven Stukas of I./StG 5 attacked the airfield at Vaenga some dozen miles downstream from Murmansk.

In the middle of the following month, on 15 July, the *Gruppe* was once again over Murmansk. This time it damaged the Soviet submarine *Shch-403* and the 6187-ton American freighter *Yaka*, the latter recently arrived in port with convoy PQ 14. And 48 hours later it was mounting yet another attack on the railway to the south, this time in the Kandalaksha area, where the Ju 87s skirted the shores of the White Sea.

During the course of four small-scale raids on 1 June, I./StG 5's pilots finally accounted for the British merchantman *Empire Starlight*. This 6850-ton vessel had reached Murmansk with other survivors of PQ 13 – the first Arctic convoy to be seriously mauled at sea – at the end of March. She had suffered her first damage in a bombing raid on 3 April, and was subjected to repeated attacks thereafter – up to as many as seven a day! It was even rumoured that, for some unknown reason, she had been singled out for special attention by the Luftwaffe. The *Gruppe* also sent the Soviet freighter *Subbotnik* to the bottom on 1 June, but the day's operations had cost them one of its number. I./StG 5 lost two more machines to Red Air Force fighters over the port the following day when it damaged the submarine *Shch-404*.

On 23 June Hauptmann Arnulf Blasig relinquished command of I./StG 5 to take up a staff position in Berlin. He was replaced as *Gruppenkommandeur* by Oberleutnant Hans-Karl Stepp, a recent Knight's Cross winner and hitherto the *Staffelkapitän* of 7./StG 2. The next day Stepp's pilots caught and sank one of the Royal Navy's Russian-based ocean going minesweepers, HMS *Gossamer*, in the Kola Inlet.

For the remainder of the year I./StG 5 would, by eastern front standards, continue to lead a

An Arctic dawn. The rising sun glints off the flanks of a machine of I./StG 5 as it taxies out to take off trailing a feathery veil of powdered snow and ice in its wake

The sun may have climbed higher into the sky, but the temperatures are still sub-zero. Note the fur-hatted mechanic with the refuelling hose kneeling on the wing, the tarpaulins protecting the 'Dora's' engine and cockpit, the straw matting over the bonnet of the bowser and the cluster of bombs, complete with tail screamers, stacked carelessly – if conveniently – nose-down in the snow

remarkably static existence. Still dividing its time between the Murmansk area and the railway running south from it, the *Gruppe* would only occasionally be required to divert its strength – either partially or wholly – away from its near-permanent base at Kirkenes for brief deployments to other regions on the Arctic or Finnish fronts. But with Hitler's 1942 summer offensive commencing just four days after the unfortunate *Gossamer* had gone down in the Kola Inlet with 24 of her crew, it is now time to catch up with events on the main sectors of the front.

The Red Army's fresh Siberian divisions had kept up the pressure of their counter-attacks in front of Moscow throughout the opening weeks of 1942. The only Stukas in their path were those of *Stab* and III./StG 2 which had been wintering at Dugino, 30 miles (48 km) north of Vyazma on the Moscow highway. In mid-January these units had successfully broken up an attempted enemy breakthrough in the vicinity of Rzhev. Then, in the early hours of 18 January, it was Dugino itself that was suddenly under threat from the Red Army. An armoured spearhead was reported rapidly closing in from the north.

While staff company commander Oberleutnant Kresken wasted no time in issuing arms to the ground personnel and organising them into detachments to help strengthen the airfield's perimeter defences, *Geschwaderkommodore* Major Paul-Werner Hozzel and his pilots were forced to wait for first light before being able to take off to engage the approaching enemy tanks;

'It was now a matter of flying to hold the field and "protect our own hides". Operations were short, mostly of no more than 15 minutes' duration – take-off, land, reload, take-off. A few tanks managed to get through almost as far as the perimeter, but they were seen off by our anti-tank and heavy flak guns.'

Dugino's motley crew of defenders held out for 72 hours before a task force despatched by 2. *SS-Panzerdivision 'Das Reich'* arrived to drive the Soviets back and restore the situation. Despite close calls such as this, the Red Army's counter-attacks along the Moscow front made little headway against the entrenched German positions, and in mid-February they ground to a halt altogether.

But things were very different on Army Group Centre's left flank up to, and beyond, its boundary with Army Group North. In these areas, a series of Soviet counter-offensives had not merely threatened various points along the front, they had actually succeeded in encircling considerable numbers of German troops in several 'pockets'. It was on 18 January, the day StG 2 had been attacked at Dugino, that the ring had closed around the largest enclave of all – that at Demyansk, southeast of Lake Ilmen – trapping 95,000 German troops.

The boot had been firmly transferred to the other foot. The 'cauldrons' of 1941 had become the 'pockets' of 1942, and it was German troops who were now cut off and facing surrender or annihilation. But Hitler had other ideas. He promptly declared Demyansk, and the much smaller encirclement at Cholm, some 60 miles (96 km) to the southwest, to be *Feste Plätze* (literally 'firm places', i.e. strongholds). They were to be supplied with food and ammunition by air until such time as they could be relieved, and then used as jumping-off points for renewed attacks on the Red Army.

As *Luftflotte* 1 (the air fleet responsible for Army Group North's area of operations) had no dive-bomber units of its own, *Stukagruppen* had to be transferred in from elsewhere to support the ground fighting around the hotly contested pockets. The first to arrive was I./StG 2, hastily recalled from its period of rest and re-equipment in Germany. The unit's brand new Ju 87Ds touched down at Dno, roughly equidistant from both Demyansk and Cholm, on 19 January.

The Stukas quickly proved their value, not only during the fierce fighting around the two pockets, but also in helping to repel another Red Army offensive that was attempting to smash through the frontlines at nearby Staraya Russa – an important road and rail junction just to the south of Lake Ilmen.

Although I./StG 2's new *Doras* were undoubtedly an improvement on the unit's earlier Ju 87Bs, they were still just as vulnerable to one of the Stuka pilot's most dangerous enemies – well-directed anti-aircraft fire. On 12 February, the machine being flown by the *Gruppe's* recently appointed *Kommandeur*, Hauptmann Bruno Dilley (who, incidentally, had led the very first Stuka operation of the war, as detailed in *Osprey Combat Aircraft 1* on pages 20-21), took a direct hit during a low-level attack behind enemy lines well to the east of Staraya Russa. An emergency landing ended in the aircraft's somersaulting and an unconscious Dilley being dragged from the cockpit by his wireless-operator/gunner, Oberfeldwebel Kather. For the next three days and nights the pair dodged Soviet troops and battled freezing temperatures before finally reaching the friendly haven of the Demyansk pocket. It was not the last time the intrepid duo would return on foot from deep inside enemy territory.

Early in February, *Luftflotte* 1's Stuka establishment had been doubled by the arrival of III./StG 1, also newly returned from refurbishment in the Reich. But even with their combined strength of 50+ *Doras*, I./StG 2 and III./StG 1 found themselves hard pressed to answer all the demands being made upon them as the fighting continued to rage around the Demyansk and Cholm pockets.

There were some spectacular successes. On one occasion in February, I./StG 2's pilots were asked to deal with a particularly troublesome armoured train that was operating along the Staraya Russa line down to the east of Demyansk in support of the Red Army's latest attempt to collapse the pocket. The Stuka crews displayed their 'flying artillery' skills to the

Hauptmann Bruno Dilley, the *Gruppenkommandeur* of I./StG 2, climbs out of the cockpit, map in hand. Dilley, who had led the very first Stuka mission of the war, would have to fly 324 more before being awarded the Knight's Cross in June 1942

A machine of 9./StG 1 emerges from its snow-bound dispersal. The white winter camouflage is already showing signs of considerable wear and tear – the heavy exhaust staining across the wing root, the result of the different fuel/air mixture required for cold weather operations, is particularly noticeable

full. All six of the white-camouflaged, heavily armoured wagons of the train were derailed, with two tipped completely over on their sides and the rest left leaning drunkenly across the tracks.

The dive-bombers brought succour to the ground troops in other ways too. Quite literally so, in fact, for whereas Demyansk boasted an airstrip within its perimeter on which relays of Ju 52/3m transports were able to land with much needed supplies, the 3500 defenders of Cholm enjoyed no such luxury. They were reliant on air drops alone. And the Stukas, with their legendary reputation for pinpoint accuracy, were often called upon to perform such missions, delivering supplies to specific units within the limited confines of the Cholm pocket.

Gradually, however, the battles for the two pockets began to ease (Demyansk would finally be relieved on 21 April and Cholm exactly a fortnight later) as the Red Army concentrated its efforts instead on exploiting the breakthrough it had achieved along the line of the River Volkhov, which flowed northwards from Lake Ilmen to Lake Ladoga, the large body of water to the east of Leningrad.

During March, the focus of air activity also naturally turned to those areas where the ground fighting was fiercest. On 16 March 3./StG 2 lost their *Staffelkapitän*, Oberleutnant Friedrich Platzer, when engine damage forced him to make an emergency landing near Lake Ilmen. In so doing, the machine ran into a ditch and overturned, killing both crewmembers. The long-serving Platzer, with nearly 400 missions to his credit, received a posthumous Knight's Cross and promotion to Hauptmann on 5 April.

March also saw a third *Stukagruppe* added to *Luftflotte* 1's northern sector order of battle. Yet another to come straight from the homeland, this was the newly re-formed II./StG 2 under the command of Hauptmann Dr Ernst Kupfer. The unit's combat debut on the Volkhov front was not altogether auspicious. Returning from one of its first missions, II./StG 2 was bounced by Red Air Force machines as it was preparing to land back at base and six of its *Doras* were either destroyed or severely damaged.

Towards the end of March air operations moved further north still – all the way up to Leningrad itself, in fact – when the decision was taken to mount another onslaught on the capital ships of the Soviet Baltic Fleet before the last of the winter ice broke up and allowed them access to open water. Or, as the order from *Luftflotte* 1 phrased it, 'Attacks on the Soviet major warships in the Kronstadt-Leningrad harbour areas and destruction of the Soviet flak emplacements'.

Among the aircraft assembled for Operation *Eisstoss* ('Ice-thrust') were the 62 *Doras* of III./StG 1 and II./StG 2. The first mission was flown on 4 April, and although the Stukas' escorting Messerschmitts were able to keep enemy fighters at bay, Leningrad's ferocious anti-

Fully-loaded, these 'Dora's' of 4./StG 2 – 'T6+KM' in the foreground – are setting off for another mission on the northern sector. Although there is no longer any need for winter camouflage, the wheel-spats have been removed in deference to spring's all-pervading mud. Note the white segment at the top of the rudder of 'BM', the second aircraft in the formation

aircraft defences prevented the dive-bombers from inflicting any severe damage. One bomb hit the cruiser *Kirov*, but it failed to explode. Near misses did, however, cause some minor damage to the battleship *Oktyabrskaya Revolutsiya*, another cruiser and several smaller vessels. A follow-up attack that same night by He 111 bombers produced no results whatsoever. It was clear that *Eisstoss* had not been a success.

As in the previous autumn's raids on Kronstadt, it was decided that heavier bombs were the answer, and these were promptly sent for. They would not arrive for nearly three weeks, and it was 24 April before the raids resumed, this time under the code-name of Operation *Götz von Berlichingen* (a 16th-century warrior knight with an artificial iron hand, who inspired a famous novel and whose name, for reasons which need not be gone into here, equates to 'Kiss my ass').

The 24 April raid fared little better than *Eisstoss*. The cruiser *Kirov* took two more direct hits, which this time detonated with considerable loss of life, while the *Oktyabrskaya Revolutsiya* sustained further slight damage from another near miss. One Stuka was shot down and the pilot of another, I./StG 2's Leutnant Herbert Bauer, was severely wounded when a machine gun bullet shattered his jaw. Despite his appalling injuries, Bauer managed to land his machine at a forward field only some 16 miles (25 km) south of Leningrad, and he would recover to win both the Knight's Cross and Oak Leaves as a *Schlacht* pilot later in the war.

Twenty-four hours later 40 Ju 87s were unable to penetrate the anti-aircraft barrage around Leningrad and, after tangling with Soviet fighters, were fortunate to return to base at Krasnogvardeisk without loss. The last day of April witnessed the final raid, reportedly carried out by just three aircraft. The battle between the Stukas and the Soviet Baltic Fleet had ended not with a bang, but with a whimper. And it was shortly after this, early in May, that the whole of StG 2, with the exception of one *Staffel*, was ordered back to the Reich. I. and II. *Gruppen* were subsequently withdrawn from the Leningrad and Volkhov fronts.

At the same time III./StG 2, after making the short hop from Dugino to Vyazma in February, and having continued to operate in front of Moscow since, was pulled back from the central sector – via brief stopovers at Smolensk and Vitebsk – to join the rest of the *Geschwader* at airfields in the Vienna-Graz areas of Austria.

This meant that along the more than 1200 miles (1950 km) of tortuously winding frontline that made up the northern and central sectors at this stage of the war there were now just two *Stukagruppen* in action – II. and III./StG 1. After the abortive second series of raids on the Soviet Baltic Fleet, III. *Gruppe* was transferred back down to the Demyansk-Cholm regions, where the Red Army was again pressing hard. Throughout this time III./StG 1's casualty lists were growing steadily longer. Over a dozen crews were lost and many more aircraft were written off or damaged. Most of the losses were the result of anti-aircraft fire, with only two of the *Gruppe's* machines being shot down by Soviet fighters.

Meanwhile, II./StG 1 continued to hold the fort on the central sector. This unit had maintained a presence at Sezhchinskaya, southwest of Moscow, for much of the winter while elements were rotated back to Germany for rest and re-equipment. At full strength again by mid-February, II./StG 1 helped repulse a number of local counter-attacks

Near misses surround the ancient battleship *Oktyabrskaya Revolutsiya*, moored in Kronstadt's outer harbour (bottom), during the Stukas' second series of strikes against the Soviet Baltic Fleet in the spring of 1942

during the spring as Soviet troops tried anew to drive the invaders back from their capital city. Despite the high level of operational activity, the *Gruppe* sustained relatively few casualties. But its luck was to run out on 21 May.

The target on this date was an important bridge on one of the Red Army's main supply routes west out of Moscow. The Stukas were led by acting Kommandeur Hauptmann Robert-Georg *Freiherr* von Malapert-Neufville. It was his 510th operational mission of the war.

Von Malapert-Neufville was credited with destroying the bridge, scoring a direct hit in a 'daring low-level attack'. But a burst of anti-aircraft fire had fractured his radiator and, with the oil temperature already off the clock, he had to make an immediate emergency landing. Reports indicate that he put the stricken aircraft down in no-man's land. Both von Malapert-Neufville and his air-gunner, Oberfeldwebel Otto Mees, survived and set about getting back to the German lines, unaware that they were being observed. When von Malapert-Neufville raised himself from the ground to make the final dash for safety he was shot through the head by a Soviet sniper.

Otto Mees got through, however, and an infantry squad went out to recover his pilot's body. Hauptmann von Malapert-Neufville, who was laid to rest at Sezhchinskaya, had been awarded the Knight's Cross back in January. He would be honoured with posthumous Oak Leaves on 8 June.

Elsewhere significant changes were taking place. The reason for StG 2's second return to the Reich in the space of just six months had again been for purposes of re-equipment. The *Geschwader's* recent front-line role as a 'mobile fire brigade' had been imposed upon it by force of circumstances – the inadequate number of *Stukagruppen* in the east, the immense areas to be covered and the growing strength of the enemy.

But what had started out as a temporary local expedient was now adopted as official policy. The Luftwaffe High Command recognised that the most effective way of utilising the few *Stukagruppen* it was deploying against the Soviet Union would be to convert them into self-contained, mobile fighting units able to transfer at a moment's notice to any point along the front without having to call upon transport aircraft to ferry their essential equipment and ground staffs. The *Transportgruppen* themselves were already beginning to be stretched beyond their limit, as witness the enforced use of school machines, flown by instructors, in the recent Demyansk and Cholm airlifts.

Thus, when StG 2 returned to the eastern front in mid-June it had been supplied with the equipment necessary to enable it to fulfil its new mobile role. Over a quarter of its *Doras* were now fitted with tailhooks, and the *Geschwader* had some 40 transport gliders of its own, making it, in effect, an independent rapid redeployment force.

While undergoing maintenance, an aircraft of 8./StG 1 shares a fairly substantial wooden hangar with a Ju 88 (foreground right). The northern areas were far more stable than the volatile southern sector, and those units attached – however briefly – to *Luftflotte* 1 often enjoyed the luxury of a semi-permanent base such as this

StG 2 was not heading back to the central sector, however. Hitler had seemingly lost interest in Moscow. His attention was now focused on a far more practical and valuable prize – the oilfields of the Caucasus far to the southeast. This was to be the objective for the Wehrmacht's 1942 summer offensive, code-named Operation *Blau* (Blue).

Having staged from Austria, via the Protectorate and Poland, to Zhitomir, in the Ukraine, the *Geschwader* then 'dribbled' its aircraft a *Kette* (three machines) at a time along the last lap to its assigned forward ground to the east of Kursk in the hope that this would conceal their arrival from the enemy. Whether the ploy worked or not is uncertain. What is beyond doubt is that the opening stages of the 1942 offensive were highly successful.

Launched on 28 June, Operation *Blau* began in tried and tested fashion, with two armies smashing through the Soviet frontlines in a giant pincer movement to the east and southeast of Kursk. Their immediate objective was the important town of Voronezh. StG 2 not only supported the Panzers' 90 mile (145 km) advance on Voronezh, they also threw their entire strength – more than 120 Stukas in all – in a raid against the town itself, where four armaments factories were reported to be still working at full stretch.

The 45 machines of the *Geschwaderstab* and I. *Gruppe* attacked the primary target – a tank manufacturing plant – while the remaining six *Staffeln* were divided between the other three factories, one turning out artillery pieces and two producing munitions. All four targets were severely damaged by the Stukas' 500-kg and 50-kg high-explosive bombs, and all aircraft returned to base without loss. They had not encountered a single Soviet fighter over Voronezh. Nor had the town's anti-aircraft defences overly impressed StG 2's crews;

'The flak opened up at us very early, but it didn't bother us all that much as we had experienced, and survived, a lot worse over Kronstadt.'

Despite such undoubted successes in the air, events on the ground were no longer going strictly according to plan. Voronezh was taken on 6 July and the pincer movement completed. But the resulting 'cauldron' was almost empty. The Red Army had learned from its mistakes of the previous summer. No longer were its troops being ordered to 'stand fast at all costs', thereby allowing themselves to be encircled and either annihilated or captured.

The divisions of the Soviet Bryansk and Southwest Fronts had deliberately disengaged and withdrawn eastwards in the face of the advancing Axis forces. Stalin, who had been paranoid about forfeiting even an inch of ground to the enemy 12 months earlier, was now confident enough to realise that temporary loss of territory – something the USSR was hardly short of – was not going to be harmful to his pursuance of the war in the longer term.

The Red Army's prolific use of armoured trains made them a frequent target for the Luftwaffe's Stukas. This one, with several of its wagons still blazing fiercely, was knocked out by StG 2 east of Maryino on 28 June – the opening day of Operation *Blau*

Aircraft of the *Gruppenstab* StG 2 in the summer of 1942. The nearest machine's fuselage code, 'T6+BC', and the numeral '2' on the wheel-spat, points to it being the mount of either the unit's adjutant or operations officer. Note the name *Bärli* ('Teddy bear') on the engine cowling – but this is *not* the same *Bärli* as that depicted by colour Profile 13. The likeliest candidate for pilot of both machines is Leutnant Günther Schmid, who is known to have served as Hauptmann Dr Kupfer's *Gruppenadjutant* before taking over as *Staffelkapitän* of 5./StG 2 in late 1942

Hitler, on the other hand, regarded the Red Army's latest retreat as a sure sign that he was winning the war in the east. Declaring yet again that 'the enemy is defeated', he promptly expanded the aims of his 1942 summer offensive. Operation *Blau*, which had already metamorphosed into Operation *Braunschweig* (Brunswick) within 48 hours of its launch, was now divided into two entirely separate parts. While Army Group 'A' was directed to advance southeast down into the Caucasus, Army Group 'B' was ordered to strike due east towards Stalingrad.

Air Fleet 4, responsible for the whole of the southern sector, had, of necessity, to split its own forces in two as well. Its IV. *Fliegerkorps*, which included the Stukas of StG 77 recently withdrawn from the fighting around Sevastopol, would support the push into the Caucasus. VIII. *Fliegerkorps*, to which StG 2 had now returned, was to accompany the advance on Stalingrad. Hitler spelled out the part the Luftwaffe was to play in his *Führer* Directive No 45, dated 23 July 1942;

'The task of the Luftwaffe is, primarily, to give strong support to the land forces crossing the Don and to concentrate its forces on the destruction of the Timoshenko Army Group (i.e. the Soviet Southwest Front). In addition, the operations of Army Group "B" against Stalingrad will be supported. The early destruction of the city of Stalingrad is especially important.

'Secondly, sufficient forces must be allocated to cooperate with the thrust on (the oilfields of) Baku. In view of the decisive importance of the Caucasus oilfields for the further prosecution of the war, air attacks on their refineries and storage tanks will only be carried out if the operations of the Army make them absolutely essential.'

In other words, Hitler was unleashing two simultaneous, but sharply diverging, advances. The further the two army groups progressed, the further apart each would be from the other. And by splitting his forces – and their air support – in this manner, the *Führer* had ensured that neither would be strong enough to attain its ultimate goal. As a recipe for certain disaster, it could hardly be bettered. And disaster is what followed, although not immediately.

After covering the southern arm of the initial Voronezh pincer offensive, the Stukas of StG 77 were next deployed in the advance on the important industrial city of Voroshilovgrad. But here, too, the bulk of the Red Army defenders disengaged and retired eastwards across the River Donets, ready and able to fight another day. The city was taken against little resistance on 19 July.

By this time the German 17. *Armee* was rapidly approaching Rostov-on-Don, the natural gateway down into the Caucasus. The city had already been captured once by 1. *Panzerarmee* back at the beginning of November 1941, but the Soviets had retaken it before that month was out. Now it was about to change hands again. The veterans of StG 77 played a large part in its fall. Just days earlier, the *Geschwader* had celebrated its 30,000th sortie since the beginning of *Barbarossa*. This achievement had resulted in *Reichsmarschall* Göring's sending of a personal message extending his heartiest congratulations.

But it was also over Rostov – on 22 July, just 24 hours before the city was recaptured – that 8./StG 77 lost its *Staffelkapitän*. Hauptmann Gerhard Bauhaus, who had been awarded the Knight's Cross two months earlier, suffered severe burns when his *Dora* was hit by anti-aircraft fire. Despite immediate hospitalisation, first in the Ukraine and then back in

In the hot sun of a Ukrainian summer servicing aircraft out in the open was no hardship at all

An impressive line-up of *'Doras'* of 3./StG 77. The bareheaded figure on the left of the group is Feldwebel Herbert Rabben, who was considered by many to be one of the best pilots ever to fly with StG 77. He would be awarded the Knight's Cross after the *Geschwader's* incorporation into the *Schlacht* arm

the Reich, the 33-year old Bauhaus would ultimately succumb to his injuries on 2 September.

On 28 July elements of StG 77 suddenly found themselves back in action against Soviet naval vessels. Their targets on this occasion, however, were not the cruisers and destroyers of the Black Sea Fleet, but a quartet of armoured motor gunboats of the Sea of Azov Flotilla which had retreated eastwards up the River Don before turning down into the Manych. The Stukas caught the gunboats near the town of Salsk, damaging three of them so severely that they were blown up by their crews to prevent them falling into the hands of the advancing Germans.

By the end of July StG 77 was based at Rostov and supporting the troops of Army Group 'A' as they broke out of their bridgeheads across the Don and began to fan southwards into the Caucasus. They made good progress at first, the towns in their path falling in quick succession. Voroshilovsk was captured on 3 August, Maykop stormed six days later and Krasnodar four days after that.

But once again communist troops were staging a fighting withdrawal, willing to relinquish the barren steppe of the central Caucasus as its forces retreated into the foothills of the Caucasus Mountains to the south. The Germans were hot on their heels. On 21 August a section of men chosen from the 1. and 4. *Gebirgsdivisionen* (Mountain Divisions) hoisted the Swastika flag atop Mount Elbrus, the highest peak in the Caucasus. Although this made good propaganda footage, providing striking images of German troops on top of Europe's highest mountain for the magazines and newsreels back home, it was of little military significance. Army Group 'A's' offensive was already running out of steam. On its right flank the Soviets were still stubbornly holding a long strip of coastline along which were situated the Black Sea Fleet's remaining bases. On the other flank, the major oilfields around Baku on the Caspian Sea were – and would remain – far out of reach.

By contrast, Army Group 'B's' advance north of the Don towards Stalingrad was gaining both in momentum and importance. In its shadow the fighting in the Caucasus became little more than a sideshow. The secondary nature of the latter campaign was underlined by the reduction in Army Group 'A's' air support. I./StG 77 had already been transferred to the Stalingrad front 24 hours prior to the symbolic flag-raising ceremony on Mount Elbrus. And before the end of August both the *Geschwaderstab* and II./StG 77 would be withdrawn from Taganrog for rest and re-equipment. To compensate for these departures, a single *Staffel* flew in to join III./StG 77 in the Caucasus.

A beaming Hauptmann Otto Schmidt, *Staffelkapitän* of 7./StG 77, photographed with his air-gunner after completing his 500th operational mission on 22 August 1942. Note the suitably decorated *'Berta'* in the background. On its cowling is the name *Heinz Bumke*, the aircraft having been named after a 7.*Staffel* pilot who had been killed on 15 October 1941. It was a not an uncommon practice for Stuka pilots to decorate their aircraft with the names of fallen comrades

1942 – ROAD TO ARMAGEDDON

While Otto Schmidt (on page 47) had to be content with a commemorative scroll, Oberleutnant Armin Thiede, the *Staffelkapitän* of 2./StG 2 – who had won his Knight's Cross prior to *Barbarossa* – was presented with a live goose upon reaching his 400th mission. The unfortunate bird probably ended up in the oven. But for the less gastronomically minded, the points of interest here are the additional armour plating on the cockpit side panels of the *'Dora'*, and the yellow stripes on the tail of the 500-kg (1100-lb) bomb in the foreground, indicating it to be a general-purpose high explosive (HE) weapon, rather than one that was armour-piercing

With the Caucasus Mountains stretching away into the distance behind them, two machines of StG 77 head back to base after a late afternoon raid

This unit was led by no less a pilot than Oberleutnant Hans-Ulrich Rudel, who, having returned to Austria to take command of the *Ergänzungsstaffel* StG 2 back in March, had by now succeeded in getting the *Staffel* moved to Sarabuz, in the Crimea, so as to be closer to the fighting. And, according to his own account, it was also at Rudel's instigation that the training *Staffel* was then transferred in mid-August to a forward landing field near Maykop so that it could participate in operations over the Caucasus.

Despite its war-weary school machines being at a 'noticeable disadvantage' when ordered to fly at high altitudes in formation with StG 77's newer *Doras*, the *Ergänzungsstaffel* gave a good account of itself. It participated in a number of raids on the Soviet Black Sea's main naval base at Tuapse, with Rudel also commenting disparagingly on the port's flak defences when compared to those of the Baltic Fleet at Kronstadt. The *Staffel* also played cat-and-mouse with an armoured train that would periodically emerge from a tunnel in a mountain valley close to Tuapse and lob a few shells at the surrounding German positions before retiring back into its lair. Its activities were finally brought to a halt when a well-placed bomb sealed the tunnel's mouth.

In September the *Ergänzungsstaffel* transferred briefly from its field at Belorechenskaya, near Maykop, to Soldatskaya, in the eastern part of the Caucasus, where it supported the ground forces fighting along the River Terek line. Rudel was hugely impressed by the majestic grandeur of the Caucasus Mountains, commenting that any one of the range's larger valleys could 'easily accommodate several of the Alps'. Back in the Maykop area, Oberleutnant Rudel clocked up his 500th operational mission on 24 September.

Aerial activity was not all one-sided, however. The Red Air Force was beginning to strike back with increasing vigour. Returning from an operation on 12 October, Rudel landed at Belorechenskaya only to find himself caught up in the middle of a raid. Luckily he was uninjured. The *Kommodore* of StG 77, recently returned with his *Geschwaderstab* from Taganrog, was not so fortunate. Major Alfons Orthofer was sitting strapped in the cockpit of his aircraft waiting to take off when the Soviet bombers struck. Seriously wounded by bomb fragments, he died in Maykop hospital later that same day.

Alfons 'Ali' Orthofer, one of the leading lights of the *Stukawaffe*, had taken over at the head of StG 77 from the long-serving Clemens *Graf* von Schönborn-Wiesentheid less than three months earlier. He was in turn replaced by another Stuka veteran, Major Walter Enneccerus.

It was shortly after this that Rudel came down with jaundice and was himself hospitalised in Rostov. The *Ergänzungsstaffel* was then pulled out of the Caucasus and transferred to Nikolayev-East, in the Ukraine.

Although Army Group 'A's foray down into the Caucasus had failed to attain its objectives, it had captured a lot of new ground. The same could not be said of the northern sector, where the front was to remain virtually static throughout most of the summer of 1942 and beyond. Lack of movement did not mean a dearth of operational activity, however. Far from it. As the only *Stukagruppe* in action along this stretch of the front, III/StG 1 was still being hard pressed to meet its many commitments. The steady toll of casualties suffered during the first half of the year began to increase, and was to include three highly experienced *Staffelkapitäne*.

By mid-July, having spent the previous few weeks shuttling back and forth attacking barges running the blockade of Lake Ladoga to ferry supplies into besieged Leningrad, blunting a Red Army drive aimed at Lyuban, and helping to keep open the still tenuous 'bottleneck' into the Demyansk pocket, III./StG 1 had returned to the Lake Ilmen area.

On 19 July Hauptmann Hartmut Schairer led his 7. *Staffel* to attack Soviet tanks reported to be approaching southeast of the lake. It was the veteran Schairer's 562nd mission of the war. But this time he was perhaps a little too confident. After his unit had successfully engaged the enemy armour, Schairer decided to make a low-level pass over the target area to assess the damage inflicted. His machine was hit by flak and crashed in flames near Staraya Russa shortly after. Both crewmen died instantly.

Schairer had won the Knight's Cross during the opening stages of *Barbarossa*. Now his long-time air-gunner, Oberfeldwebel Heinz Bevernis, who had flown with him since before the Battle of Britain, would be the first ever Stuka back-seater to receive the prestigious award – albeit posthumously, exactly two months after being killed in action.

A few days later III./StG 1 was suddenly rushed down to the Orel region of the central sector – this area having been devoid of Stukas since II/StG 1's transfer to the southern sector a month earlier – to help repulse a dangerous counter-offensive by strong enemy armoured forces. Although couched in the somewhat bombastic prose of the period, this brief extract from a contemporary magazine article gives some idea of III./StG 1's activities at this time;

'The ops room of the *Stukagruppe* is a small dilapidated wooden house that had once been the village school. A map table, two cots, a jumble of wires and cables and several field telephones fill the room. The *Staffelkapitäne* stand around the *Gruppenkommandeur* and all are concentrating on the forthcoming attack. Once again the target is Soviet tanks that are advancing towards the Orel region with all their might. This is where the Stukas will demonstrate their true worth.

'The Soviets are well camouflaged – some of the tanks have driven into farmhouses to hide themselves, so keep careful watch, look out for their tracks, and when

Oberst Walter Hagen, the *Geschwaderkommodore* of StG 1, poses for a souvenir snapshot in the summer of 1942. Note the *Geschwaderstab* badge of a diving Stuka in black on a blue shield adorning the cowling of the *'Dora'* behind him

Armourers of 7./StG 1 attach a 250-kg (550-lb) HE bomb, complete with tail screamers, to the underwing fairing of a *'Dora'*. The *Staffel's* 'winged helmet and anchor' badge is prominently displayed both on the aircraft's cowling and on the door of the Opel 'Blitz' fuel bowser behind it. Note also the yellow aft section of the wheel-spat – an innovation first introduced during III./StG 1's time in the Mediterranean

the *Staffeln* are over the target area fly one or two circuits first and don't waste your bombs. We don't get a target like this every day!

'Hauptmann Gassmann's *Stukagruppe* has fought on all fronts and has three years' combat experience behind it. Exact time now is 1145 hrs. The *Staffeln* will start to taxi at 1200 hrs. Take-off at 1205 hrs. Order of take-off eighth, seventh, ninth. Any further questions? Thank you, *meine Herren*. The briefing is over.

'The Stukas find their target. Within a few days, as well as carrying out many attacks on convoys of vehicles, infantry positions and fortified villages, the *Gruppe* has destroyed 41 tanks by direct hits and badly damaged 52 more with near misses. The Soviet offensive in the Orel area has been crushed, and a major part of this success is due to the striking power of our Stuka men.'

It was during the fighting around Orel that Oberleutnant Theodor Nordmann, the *Staffelkapitän* of 8./StG 1 who already had 50 enemy tanks to his credit, flew his 600th operational mission on 20 August. A *Staffel* diarist claims that 'Theo' Nordmann was the first Stuka pilot to reach this figure. Nordmann would survive until 1945. His two fellow-*Staffelkapitäne* in III./StG 1 were not so lucky.

After a brief stopover at Vyazma towards the end of August, the *Gruppe* was then ordered back up to the Leningrad area. And it was here on 5 September near Mga, just to the south of Lake Ladoga, that Hartmut Schairer's recent replacement at the head of 7. *Staffel* was lost. Leutnant Erich Hanne's machine, like Schairer's before it, was hit by ground fire at low level while he was attacking a group of Soviet tanks. Hanne, however, managed to regain height and nurse the crippled *Dora* back over the German lines, where he ordered his air-gunner to bail out. Before he was able to follow suit the Stuka went into a vicious spin, crashing to earth and taking the trapped Hanne with it.

And the following month, on 26 October, Hauptmann Heinz Fischer, the *Staffelkapitän* of 9./StG 1, was lost together with his air

High above a sizeable Russian town (which is presumably in German hands – note the intact bridge!), an aircraft of II./StG 1 sets off on another mission. The machine is clearly carrying 50-kg (110-lb) bomb containers underwing, but closer inspection also reveals that the ventral bomb is fitted with a sturdy *Dinortstab*, making this one of the few known photographs of such a weapon

'J9+BM' (Wk-Nr. 2312) of 7./StG 1 gets a thorough check-over between operations

gunner in a freak accident. They were carrying out a strafing run on enemy troops near Volkhov when, at a height of some 1650 ft (500 m), they inadvertently flew into the path of a German artillery shell that blew the Stuka's tail clean off. Neither crewmember managed to escape from the wildly tumbling machine, which exploded shortly before hitting the ground.

III./StG 1 was to remain on the northern sector, based mainly at Gorodez to the west of Lake Ilmen, for the rest of the year. Its last recorded loss of 1942 was an 8. *Staffel* machine shot down by Red Air Force fighters while attacking an armoured train to the east of Velikiye Luki on 30 December. By that time, however, the attention of the entire Wehrmacht was fixed on the unfolding tragedy of Stalingrad.

Initially, operations on the left-hand flank of the great summer offensive in the south had, like Army Group 'A's' drive down into the Caucasus, gone very much according to plan. On 28 June, the opening day of Operation *Blau*, General von Paulus' 6. *Armee* began its advance from the Kharkov area almost due east across the flat plains of the Don bend towards Stalingrad. Ably supported by the refurbished StG 2, and with the Red Army giving ground ahead of them, the German spearheads made rapid progress.

In order to maintain close contact with the leading armoured units, I./StG 2 was moved forward on 20 July to Tazinskaya, a town captured by 4. *Panzerarmee* just three days earlier. And on 29 July the *Geschwader* leapfrogged forward yet again, this time to Oblivskaya, a field little more than 90 miles (150 km) short of Stalingrad itself.

Although the Red Army was retreating all the while, it was still fighting as it did so. Among the casualties during this period was Hauptmann Ernst Fick, the *Staffelkapitän* of 6./StG 2, whose machine was downed on 27 July by flak near Kalach, on the River Don. July also saw the arrival on the southern sector of II./StG 1. Transferred down from the Moscow front, this *Gruppe* initially operated independently in the fighting east of Kharkov and around Taganrog, on the Sea of Azov, before joining forces with StG 2 for the advance on Stalingrad.

And the last leg of that advance was about to get under way. On 8 August the Panzer divisions of 6. *Armee* executed a pincer movement at Kalach that succeeded in trapping the bulk of two Soviet armies on the west bank of the Don. In one of the last major 'cauldron' battles of the eastern front, more than 1000 enemy tanks and armoured vehicles, together with some 750 artillery pieces, were either destroyed or captured. Eight days later the large bridge spanning the Don at Kalach was secured and the road to Stalingrad was open. General von Paulus' plan was simple. He intended to drive a corridor straight across the 40 miles (65 km) of open country that separated the Don from the River Volga and Stalingrad at

Clutching a bunch of flowers, Major Dr Ernst Kupfer, *Gruppenkommandeur* of II./StG 2, shares his cockpit with a lucky piglet upon returning to Oblivskaya after completing his 400th operational mission in August 1942. Visible in the background, right, is one of the unit's Gotha Go 242 transport gliders

this point, seal off the northern approaches to the city, and attack it in a wide right hook from the south.

To help them in their support of the ground troops, StG 2 was reinforced by both II./StG 1 and I./StG 77. The latter flew in to Oblivskaya on 20 August but, being in urgent need of rest and re-equipment following recent operations in the Caucasus, it was not to stay there long. After carrying out a number of attacks to the northwest of the city that paved the way for 16. *Panzerdivision's* advance to the Volga – which was reached on 23 July – the *Gruppe* subsequently retired to the Reich shortly afterwards. Its place on the Stalingrad front was taken by III./StG 77.

Meanwhile, 16. *Panzerdivision* was coming under severe pressure as the Red Army tried desperately to smash through the ring of steel that the Germans had thrown around the northern outskirts of the city. Oblivskaya was the scene of hectic activity during the closing days of August as I. and II./StG 2, together with II./StG 1, were in the air almost without pause in their efforts to break up the enemy's armoured counter-attacks.

They succeeded in stopping the Soviets, but the price was high. Among the casualties was the *Gruppenkommandeur* of II./StG 1. Hauptmann Johann Zemsky flew his 600th operational sortie of the war on 28 August. But there was little opportunity for the usual celebrations upon his return as another mission was scheduled almost immediately – and this time he did not come back. His machine took a direct anti-aircraft hit. Although Zemsky followed his air-gunner out of the crashing Stuka, there was insufficient altitude for his parachute to open. Zemsky's body was recovered by Fieseler *Storch* and he was buried with full military honours in the cemetery of Oblivskaya's Russian Orthodox church. A recipient of the Knight's Cross some six months earlier, Zemsky would receive posthumous Oak Leaves on 3 September.

3 September was also the day of the first massed air raid on Stalingrad itself. While the Luftwaffe's bombers set about the task of reducing the city to rubble, the Stukas were often called upon to attack specific targets. In addition to the transport gliders, StG 2 had been given its own reconnaissance *Staffel* of Bf 110s to replace an earlier *Kette* of ageing Do 17s. The Messerschmitts were used to pinpoint and photograph particularly stubborn nests of Soviet resistance – factories, apartment blocks, and the like – and the Stuka pilots would then be issued copies of these aerial photographs, suitably annotated, to augment their maps and help them locate their particular objective.

By mid-September the *Stukagruppen* had moved up to Karpovka, a gently sloping field in open country just 25 miles (40 km) outside Stalingrad. Each mission to the city was now taking less then an hour – including 15 minutes turnaround time – which meant that the crews were flying as many as eight sorties a day between sunrise and sunset. But

Mieze ('Pussycat') – aka aircraft 'T6+DC' of the *Gruppenstab* II./StG 2 – also carries additional side-armour on that partially opened canopy

A portent of things to come? Storm clouds gather and the *Dinortstäbe* on the underwing bombs of a *Gruppenstab* I./StG 2 machine (Hauptmann Bruno Dilley's 'T6+AB'?) are thrown into sharp relief against a distant rain squall – a prophetic shot taken at about the time German forces were approaching Stalingrad

as the ground troops fought their way into the centre of the city, the opposing forces became ever more closely intermixed, even to the extent of occupying different floors in the same building.

This made the Stukas' close support missions all the more difficult. Despite their large-scale maps of the city and the aerial photographs carefully marked in red ink, despite the unit leaders' aircraft being in direct radio contact with the troops below, and despite being ordered to circle several times above the target – usually indicated by ground markers or smoke – to make doubly sure before attacking, accidents could not be avoided altogether, and what today would be called 'friendly fire incidents' began to occur with increasing frequency.

The end of October saw the invaders in possession of more than two-thirds of the city. But Stalingrad's Red Army defenders, their backs to the Volga, were fighting tenaciously for every metre of ground they still held. The *Stukagruppen* were now being directed against the enemy's build-up of forces east of the Volga and to either side of Stalingrad. For whilst it was the Germans of 6. *Armee* who were locked in the bitter hand-to-hand struggle within the city itself, the sectors of the front immediately to the north and south of Stalingrad were being held by Axis satellite troops. And it was in these areas that the greatest danger threatened.

Recovered from his jaundice, Hans-Ulrich Rudel returned to frontline duty early in November as the newly-appointed *Staffelkapitän* of 1./StG 2. He wrote an account of operations at this time along the stretch of front above Stalingrad – running almost due east-west from the Volga across the open steppe to, and along, the line of the River Don – that was manned by troops of the Rumanian 3rd Army;

'At regular intervals we attack the bridges over the Don. The largest of these is located near the village of Kletskaya, where the bridgehead the Soviets have established on the west bank of the Don is constantly being extended. Every day the enemy pours more men and material across. These reinforcements are delayed, but not halted, by our destruction of the bridges around Kletskaya, as the Soviets are able to replace them relatively quickly with temporary pontoons so that the maximum flow of traffic across the river is soon fully restored.'

What Rudel and his crews were witnessing was the build-up to the main Soviet counter-offensive at Stalingrad, for it was out of the Kletskaya-Blinov bridgeheads on

After a brief period of rest and re-equipment in the Reich, I./StG 77 was soon back in action on the Stalingrad front. These three *'Doras'* – 'S2+HK' in the foreground – were photographed over the barren expanse of the Don bend *en route* to the city on 19 October 1942

Another 'HK' – this time 2./StG 2's *Leni* – takes a well-earned breather. Behind the formidable array of bombs in the foreground may be seen round-nosed bomb containers and cylindrical quadruple marker flare launchers. Both of these stores were used in abundance over Stalingrad. Note *Leni's* lack of wheel-spats and the white upper rudder segment of the machine to the rear (see also photograph on page 41)

19 November that the Red Army was to launch the assault that would encircle Stalingrad and trap the 6. *Armee*.

Most of the Luftwaffe in the Stalingrad area was immobilised by bad weather on 19 November, I./StG 2 alone being responsible for the majority of the 120 sorties flown that day. Oberleutnant Rudel again;

'After receiving an urgent message, our *Gruppe* takes off in the direction of the bridgehead at Kletskaya. The weather is bad – low lying clouds, light snow showers and the temperature probably 20 degrees below zero. We fly low. What troops are these heading towards us? We have not yet covered half the distance to the bridgehead. Masses of them in brown uniforms – are they Russians? No. Rumanians. Some are even throwing away their weapons in order to be able to run faster – a shocking sight. Prepared for the worst, we continue to fly northwards. Now we have reached our Allies' artillery positions. The guns stand abandoned, not destroyed. Their ammunition lies beside them. We fly some distance past them before we sight the first Soviet troops.'

I./StG 2 attacked the advancing Red Army units with bombs and gunfire before returning to base to rearm. But the situation was beyond saving. Despite their best efforts, the Stuka crews were unable to restore the breach torn in the Rumanian 3rd Army's lines. The Soviets continued to pour southwards past Kalach, where they joined up with the other half of the giant pincer movement that had driven through a yawning gap between Rumanian and German forces in the open steppe south of Stalingrad before wheeling northwest towards the Don. By 23 November 6. *Armee* was completely surrounded.

The *Stukagruppen* were also caught in the Soviet trap. Their main base at Karpovka lay close to the western edge of the ring the Red Army had thrown around Stalingrad. And when the Russians began tightening the noose by directing their forces inwards towards the city, Karpovka became an early target. The airfield had already been subjected to many bombing and strafing attacks during the previous weeks, and although its open expanse offered practically nothing in the way of cover, the widely dispersed machines had suffered relatively little damage.

However, on 22 November the field had faced a direct assault by a strong force of Soviet infantry backed by tanks. The resident Luftwaffe

An unfortunately rather grainy shot of Stukas over Stalingrad. The machines are flying south along the Volga almost above the point where the ferry crosses the river from the city (in the foreground) to Krasnaya Sloboda on the eastern bank

Not so much grainy as nearly invisible, this is purportedly a *'Dora'* of the *Kommando* Jungclaussen – the last Stuka unit to operate from within the Stalingrad pocket – kicking up snow as it taxies out to take off from Pitomnik

units managed to repulse the enemy temporarily, but sustained heavy losses in the process. It was clear that Karpovka could no longer be held and the Stukas were flown out to Oblivskaya 24 hours later. A small *Kommando* under the leadership of Leutnant Heinz Jungclaussen, *Staffelkapitän* of 6./StG 2, was left behind just to continue operations from other airstrips inside the pocket for as long as possible.

And although some 500 members of StG 2's ground staff were also fated to remain in Stalingrad, where they would fight on as an *ad hoc* infantry battalion, the *Geschwader* had reportedly been able to vacate Karpovka with a large number of its groundcrews and other key personnel intact. II./StG 1 was not so fortunate. Most of its support staff remained inside the pocket when the *Gruppe's* Stukas departed Karpovka, first for Oblivskaya, before then withdrawing further west to Morosovskaya. Here, after a few more days in action along the Don, the *Gruppe* would pass its remaining machines over to StG 2 early in December when its crews were ordered to retire overland to Rostov for re-equipment.

With their ring around Stalingrad snapped firmly shut, the Soviets next began to fan out westwards across the Don bend. In vacating Karpovka, StG 2's crews discovered that they had simply exchanged frying pan for fire. Their new base at Oblivskaya came under constant attack throughout 25 November. Flying a non-stop round of shuttle missions, few of which lasted more than 15 minutes, the Stukas successfully routed an entire enemy cavalry division and then managed to fend off a far more serious assault by Red Army tanks. Hans-Ulrich Rudel's logbook records a staggering 17 sorties flown on this day. But another *Staffelkapitän* was lost when 5./StG 2's Hauptmann Joachim Langbehn was brought down by anti-aircraft fire.

Yet still the enemy came on. The advance of the Red Army, which would ultimately engulf Berlin 30 months hence, gathered its first momentum west of the Don. And the Stukas were powerless to do anything about it. On 26 November I./StG 2 retired to Morosovskaya, beyond the River Chir. Twenty-four hours later II. *Gruppe*, still holding out at Marinovka, less than ten miles (15 km) west of Karpovka, beat off another Soviet attack before also withdrawing.

With both units now reduced to less than half strength, they combined forces at Morosovskaya as the *Einsatzgruppe* (Operational wing) I./StG 2. Bolstered by the machines passed over to them by the departing II./StG 1, and by the survivors of Heinz Jungclaussen's Stalingrad *Kommando*, I.(*Eins.*)/StG 2 held on grimly in the face of mounting enemy pressure while *Stab* and II./StG 2 were ordered back 200 miles (320 km) to Makeyevka, near Stalino, to begin re-equipping.

Thus, apart from the many hundreds of unfortunates among their ground personnel – including those remustered in the infantry role as the *Feldbattaillon* 'Immelmann' – the *Stukagruppen* were spared the final agonies of Stalingrad. But the epic battle for the city on the Volga, which most regard as the turning point of the war against the Soviet Union, also proved to be the watershed for the Luftwaffe's dive-bomber arm in the east. Hitherto the very epitome of *Blitzkrieg*, spreading terror and destruction as it smashed everything in its path, the Ju 87 Stuka would from now on find itself very much on the defensive.

Amidst all the carnage of the eastern front there was still time to remember Christmas. It would be nice to know if this Christmas tree tied to the ventral bomb yoke of a *'Dora'* was destined for the unit's own mess somewhere out in the steppe, or whether it was perhaps to be dropped as a gift on some isolated army outpost!

COLOUR PLATES

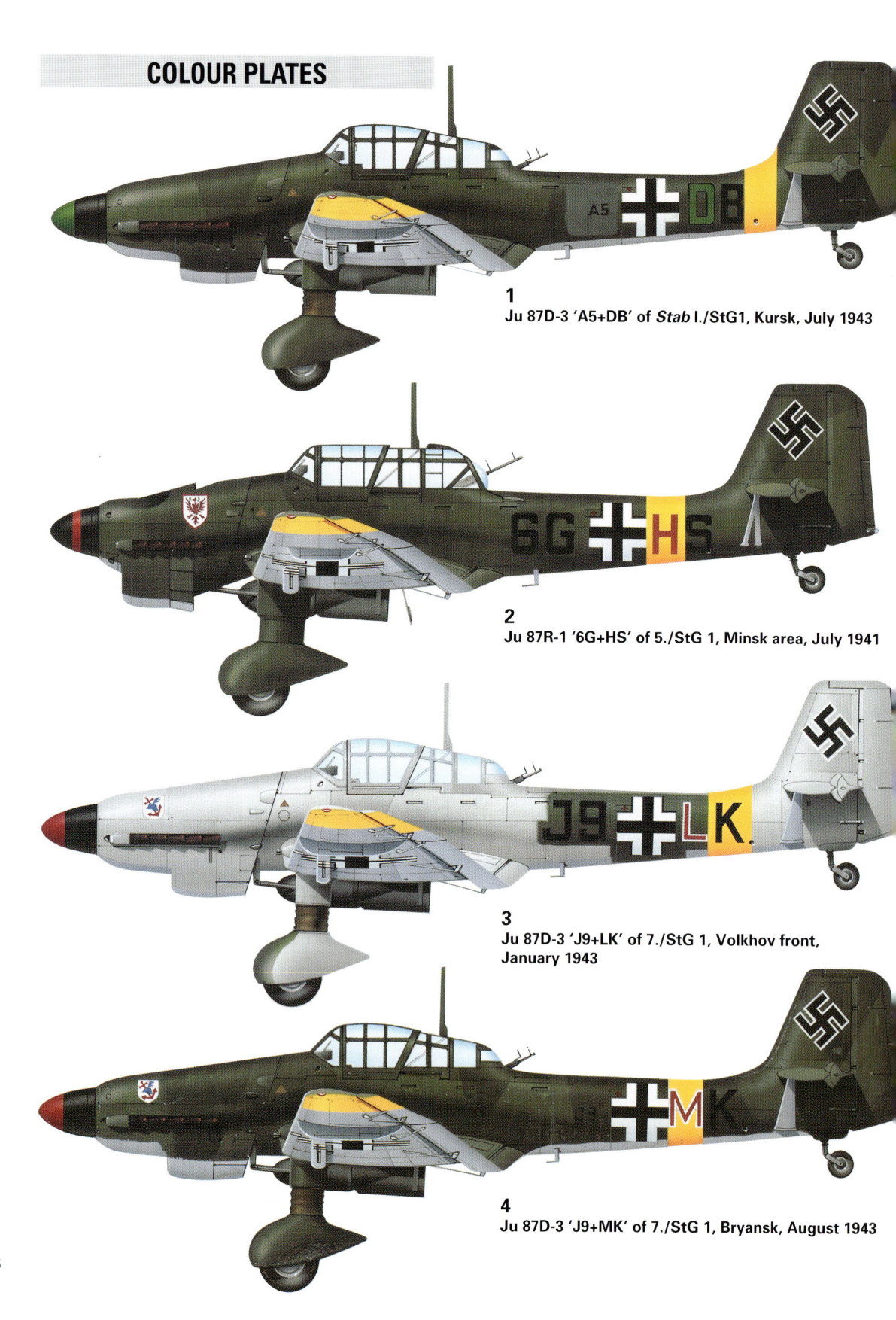

1
Ju 87D-3 'A5+DB' of *Stab* I./StG1, Kursk, July 1943

2
Ju 87R-1 '6G+HS' of 5./StG 1, Minsk area, July 1941

3
Ju 87D-3 'J9+LK' of 7./StG 1, Volkhov front, January 1943

4
Ju 87D-3 'J9+MK' of 7./StG 1, Bryansk, August 1943

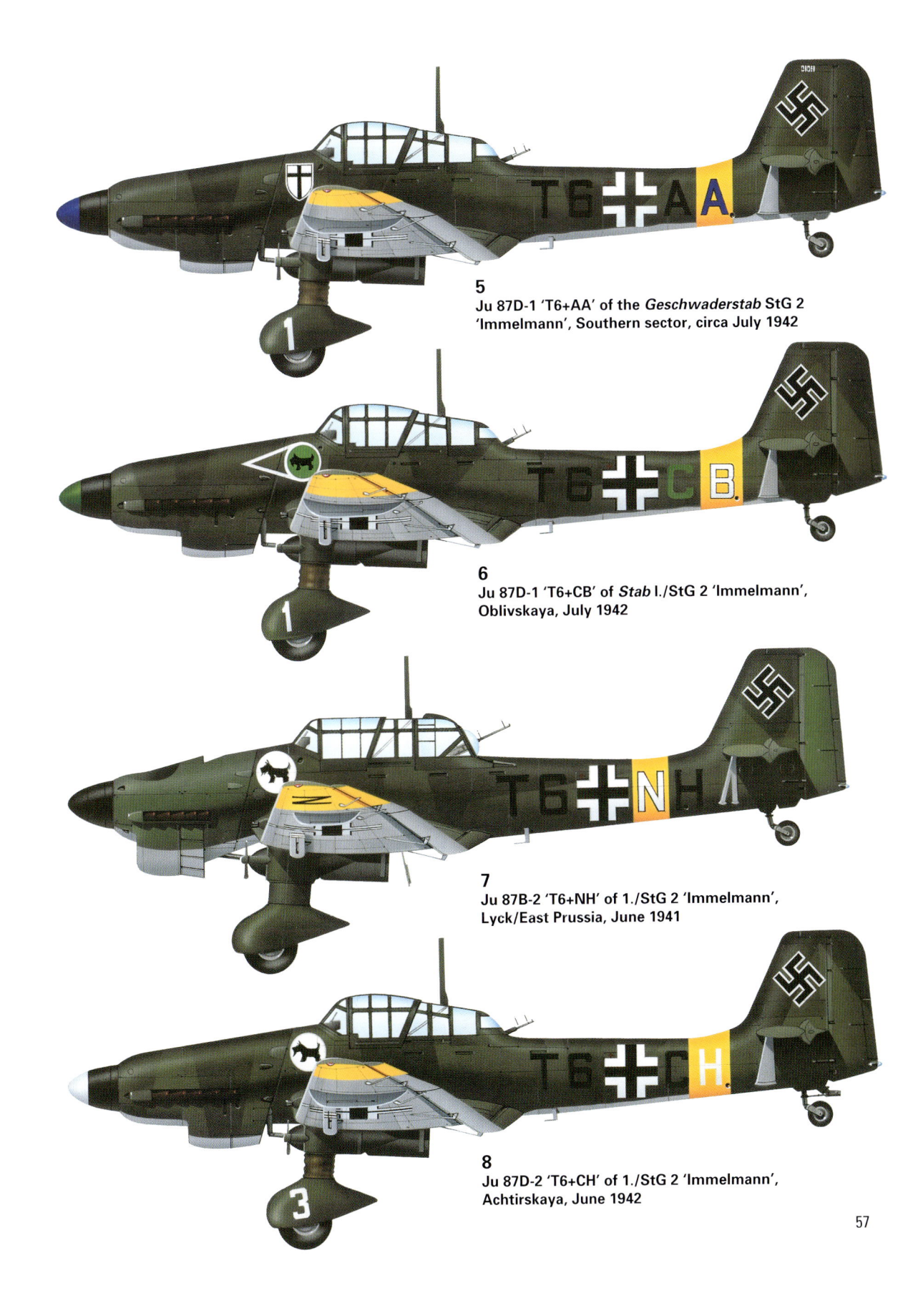

5
Ju 87D-1 'T6+AA' of the *Geschwaderstab* StG 2 'Immelmann', Southern sector, circa July 1942

6
Ju 87D-1 'T6+CB' of *Stab* I./StG 2 'Immelmann', Oblivskaya, July 1942

7
Ju 87B-2 'T6+NH' of 1./StG 2 'Immelmann', Lyck/East Prussia, June 1941

8
Ju 87D-2 'T6+CH' of 1./StG 2 'Immelmann', Achtirskaya, June 1942

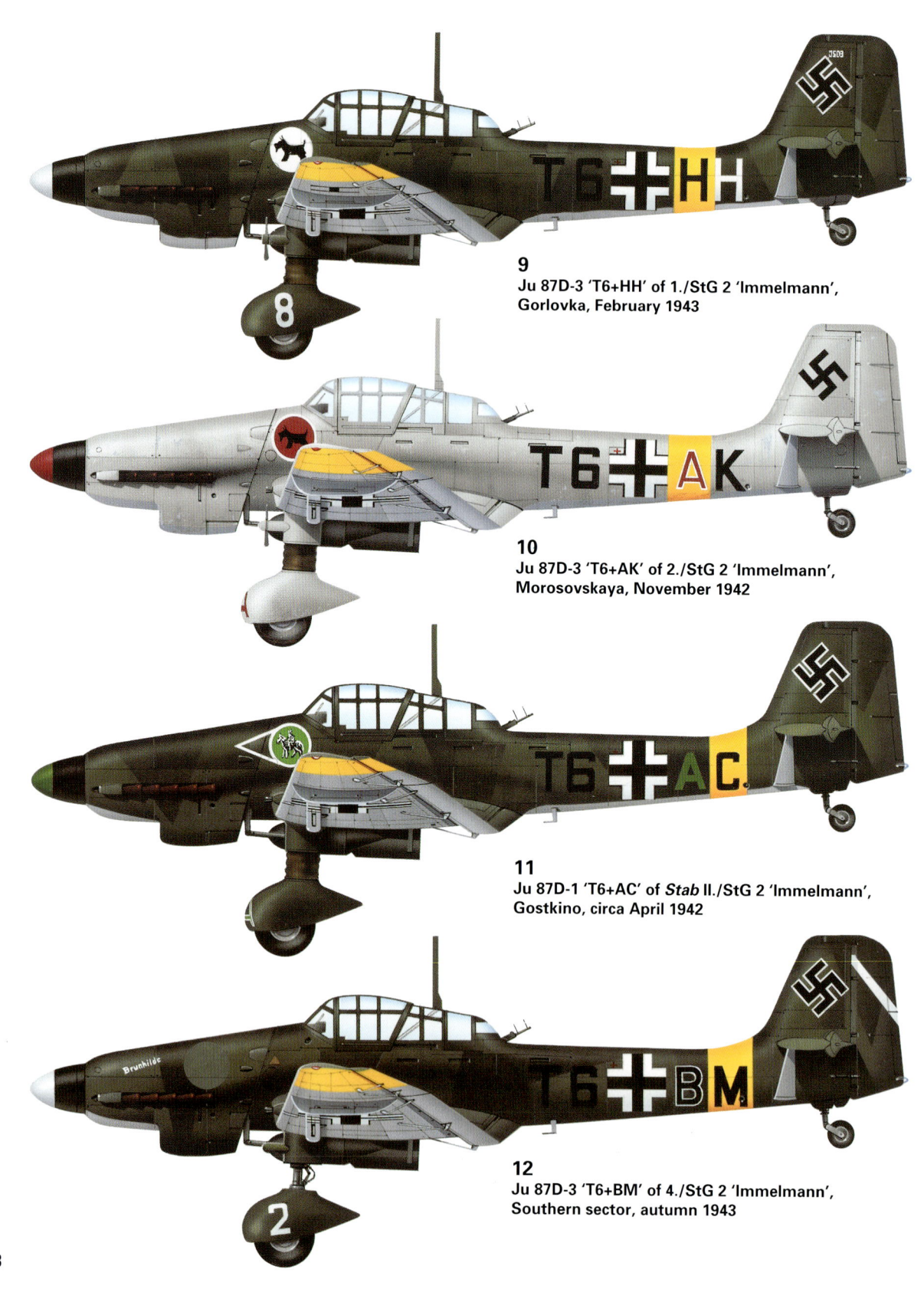

9
Ju 87D-3 'T6+HH' of 1./StG 2 'Immelmann', Gorlovka, February 1943

10
Ju 87D-3 'T6+AK' of 2./StG 2 'Immelmann', Morosovskaya, November 1942

11
Ju 87D-1 'T6+AC' of *Stab* II./StG 2 'Immelmann', Gostkino, circa April 1942

12
Ju 87D-3 'T6+BM' of 4./StG 2 'Immelmann', Southern sector, autumn 1943

58

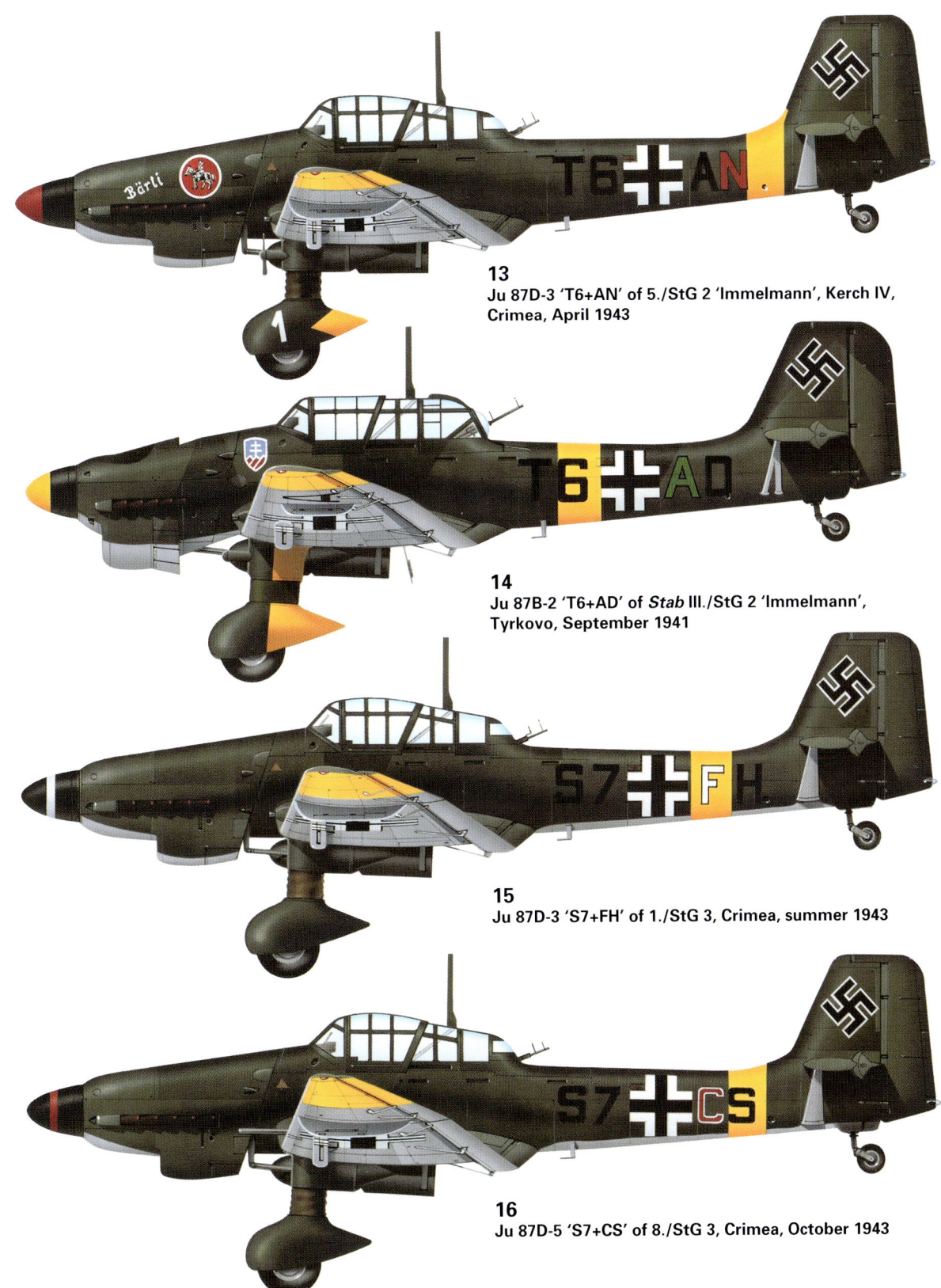

13
Ju 87D-3 'T6+AN' of 5./StG 2 'Immelmann', Kerch IV, Crimea, April 1943

14
Ju 87B-2 'T6+AD' of Stab III./StG 2 'Immelmann', Tyrkovo, September 1941

15
Ju 87D-3 'S7+FH' of 1./StG 3, Crimea, summer 1943

16
Ju 87D-5 'S7+CS' of 8./StG 3, Crimea, October 1943

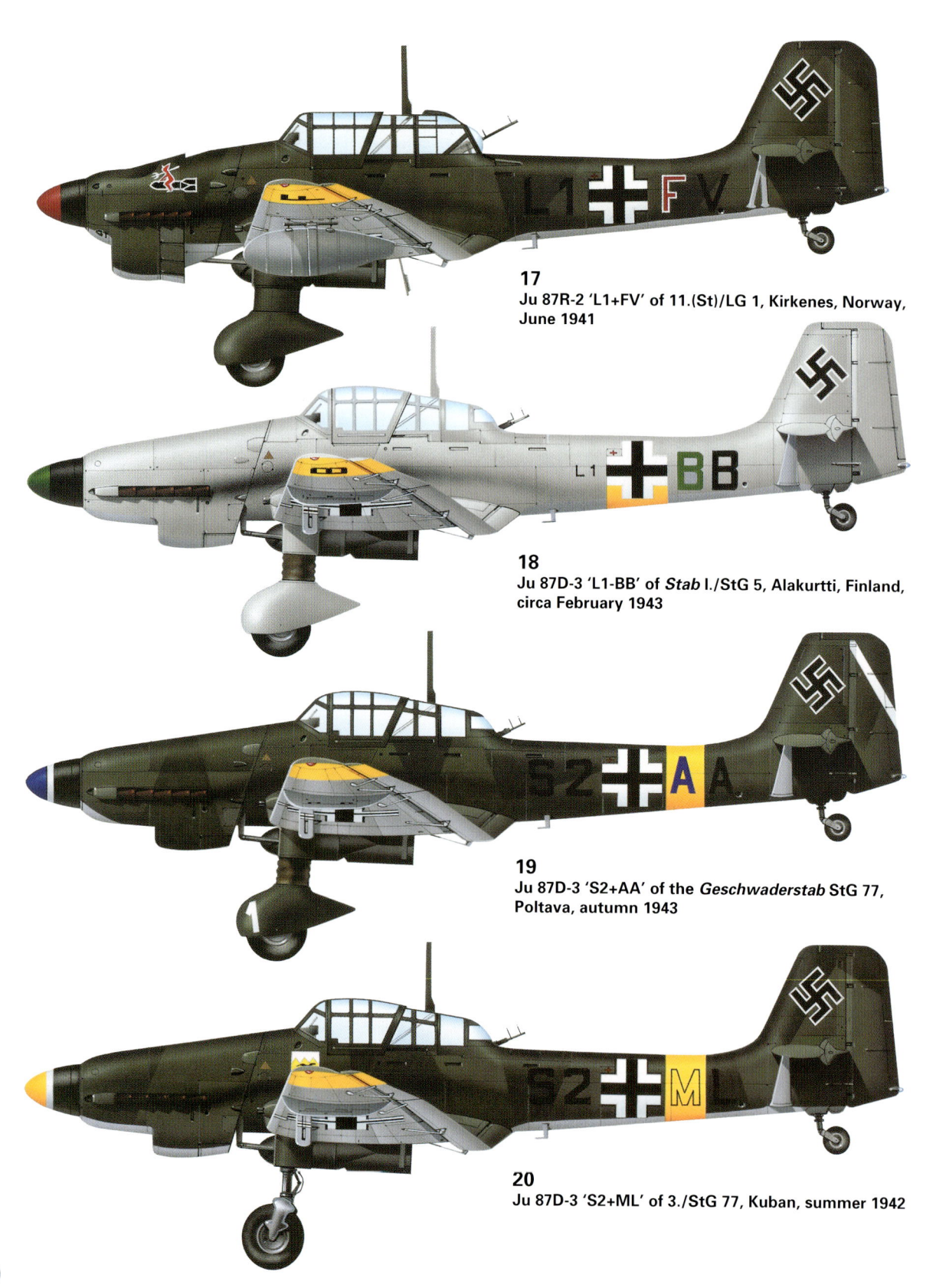

17
Ju 87R-2 'L1+FV' of 11.(St)/LG 1, Kirkenes, Norway, June 1941

18
Ju 87D-3 'L1-BB' of *Stab* I./StG 5, Alakurtti, Finland, circa February 1943

19
Ju 87D-3 'S2+AA' of the *Geschwaderstab* StG 77, Poltava, autumn 1943

20
Ju 87D-3 'S2+ML' of 3./StG 77, Kuban, summer 1942

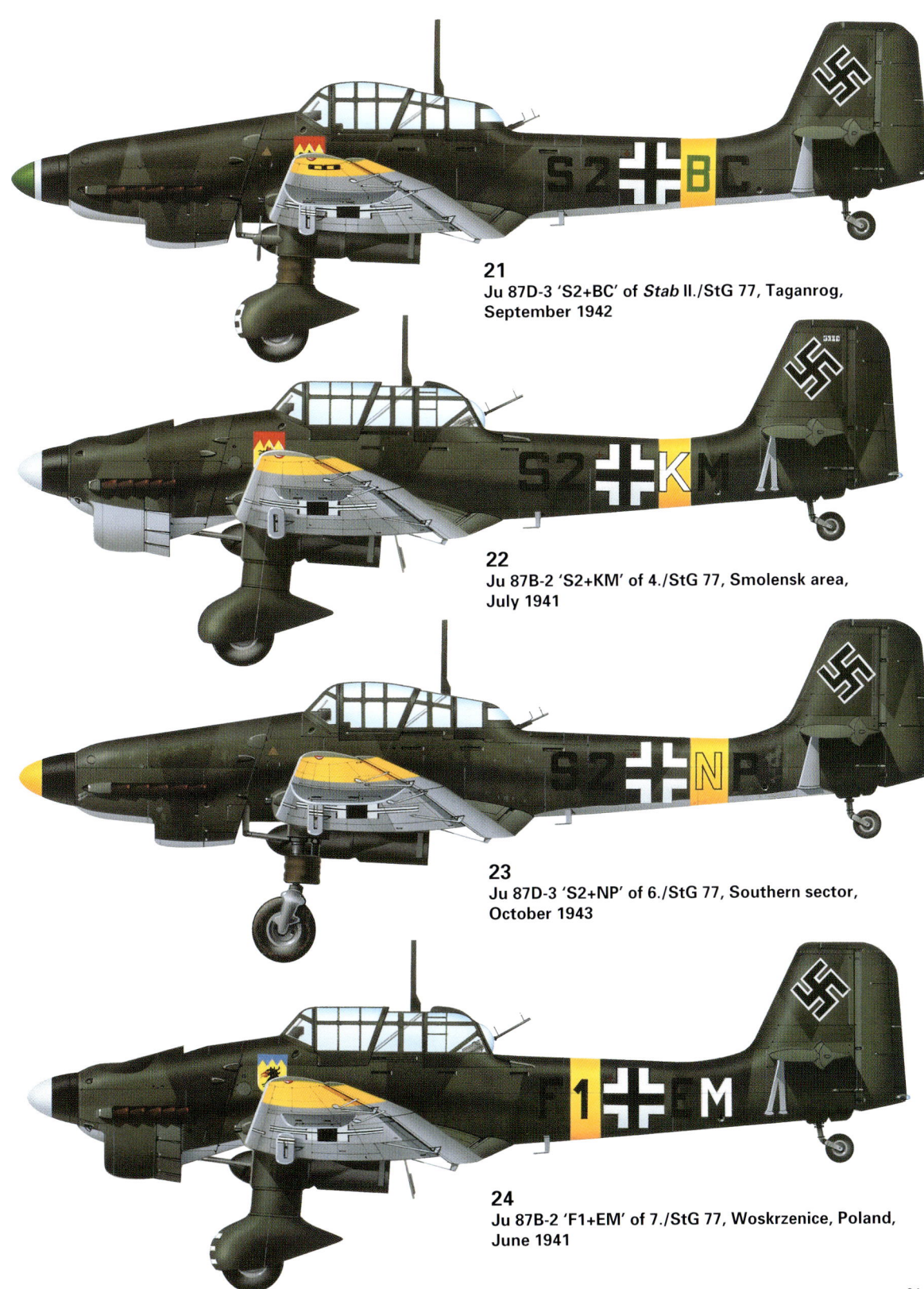

21
Ju 87D-3 'S2+BC' of *Stab* II./StG 77, Taganrog, September 1942

22
Ju 87B-2 'S2+KM' of 4./StG 77, Smolensk area, July 1941

23
Ju 87D-3 'S2+NP' of 6./StG 77, Southern sector, October 1943

24
Ju 87B-2 'F1+EM' of 7./StG 77, Woskrzenice, Poland, June 1941

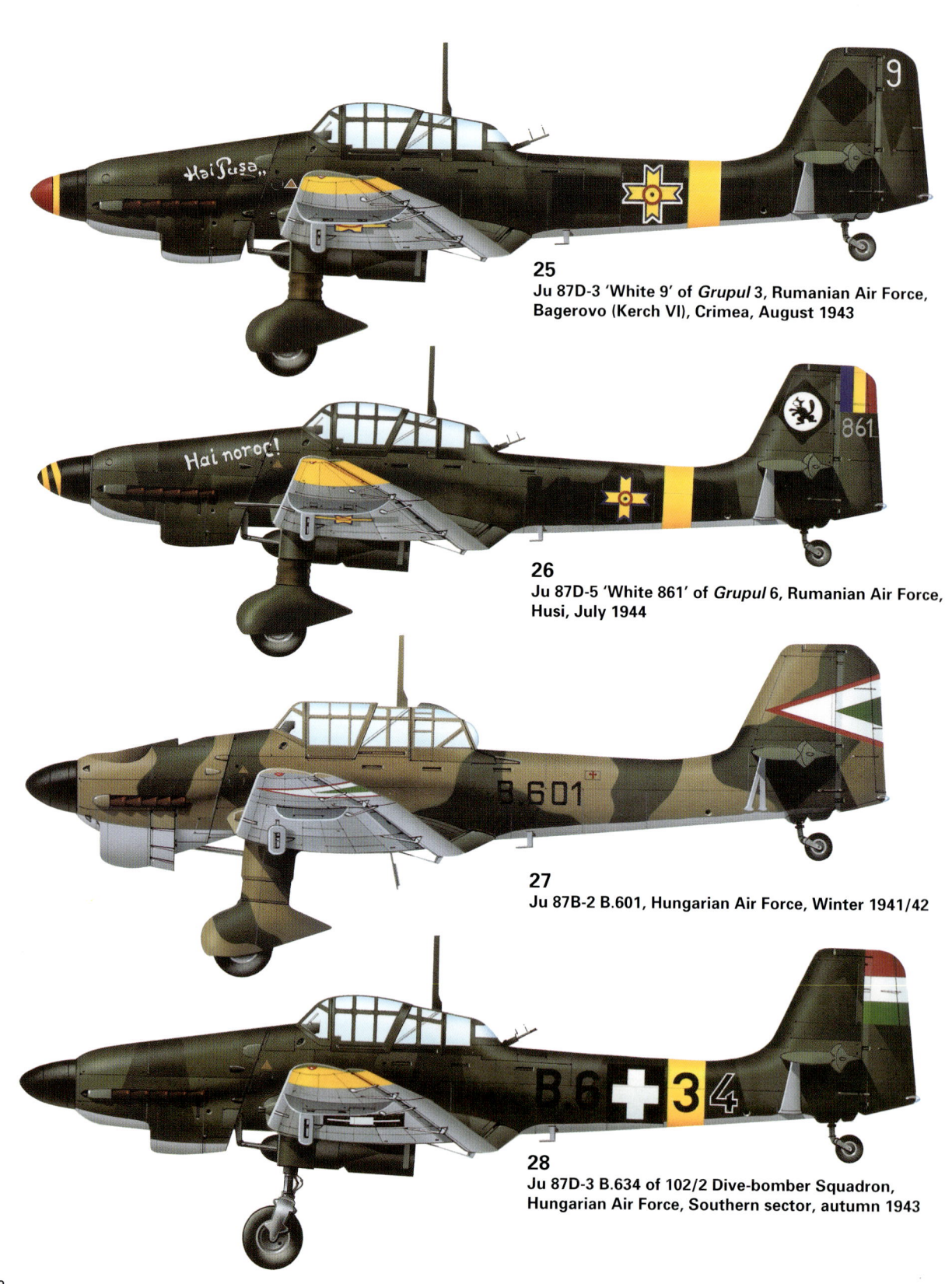

25
Ju 87D-3 'White 9' of *Grupul* 3, Rumanian Air Force, Bagerovo (Kerch VI), Crimea, August 1943

26
Ju 87D-5 'White 861' of *Grupul* 6, Rumanian Air Force, Husi, July 1944

27
Ju 87B-2 B.601, Hungarian Air Force, Winter 1941/42

28
Ju 87D-3 B.634 of 102/2 Dive-bomber Squadron, Hungarian Air Force, Southern sector, autumn 1943

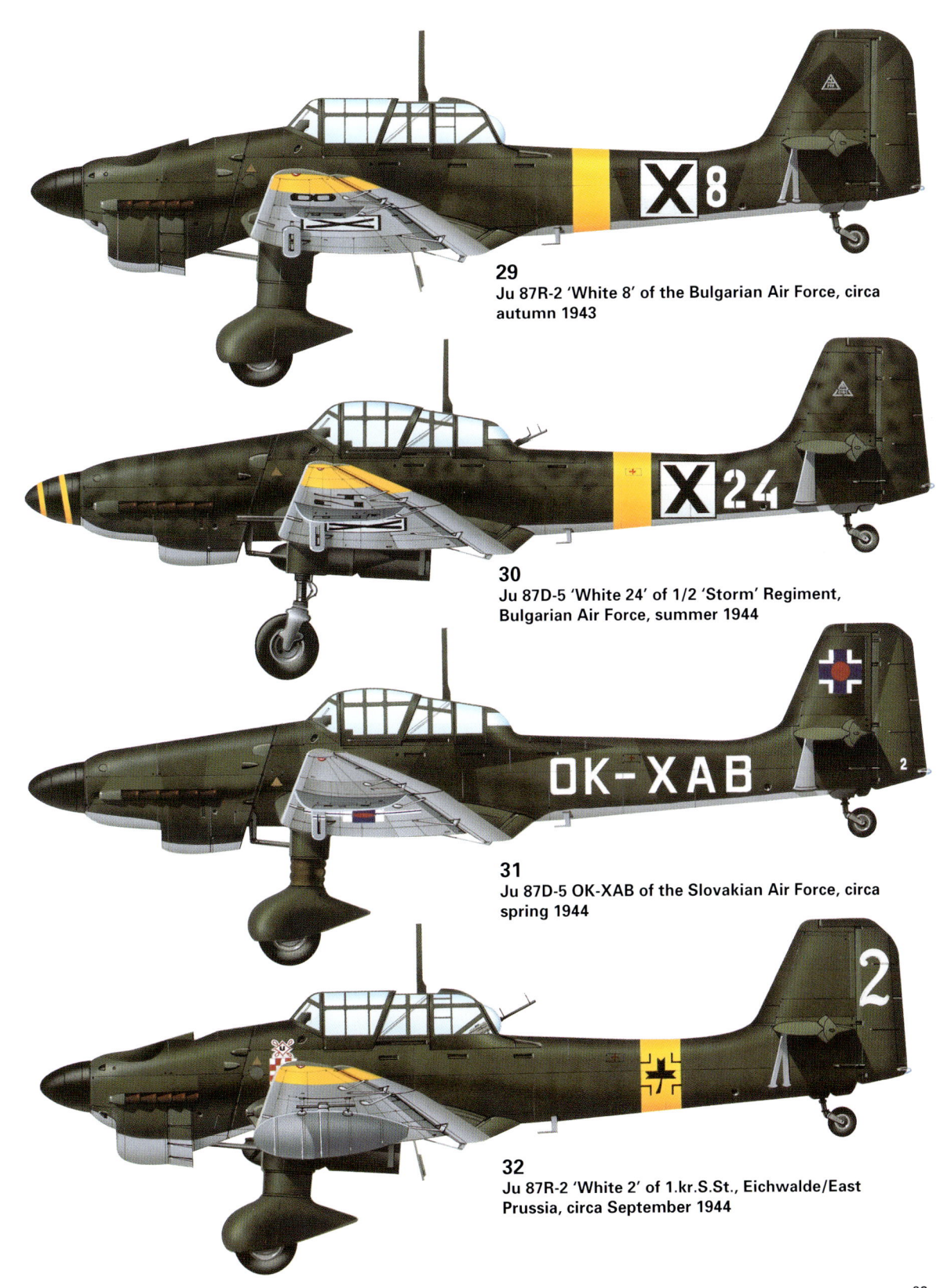

29
Ju 87R-2 'White 8' of the Bulgarian Air Force, circa autumn 1943

30
Ju 87D-5 'White 24' of 1/2 'Storm' Regiment, Bulgarian Air Force, summer 1944

31
Ju 87D-5 OK-XAB of the Slovakian Air Force, circa spring 1944

32
Ju 87R-2 'White 2' of 1.kr.S.St., Eichwalde/East Prussia, circa September 1944

63

CHAPTER THREE

1943 – YEAR OF REORGANISATION

The southern sector, which had been the scene of the *Führer's* overly-ambitious 1942 summer offensive, would also see the greatest territorial gains by the Russians early in 1943 as they began to wrest their home soil back from the Axis invaders. In the aftermath of Stalingrad – where the last remnants of 6. *Armee* laid down their arms on 2 February – Soviet forces launched a series of massive counter-attacks that would take them to, and across, one major river barrier after another.

Now it was the Germans who were retreating. But they continued to fight as they did so. Now and again they would delay, even check, the Russian juggernaut. Ground would be regained and towns retaken. Such successes were purely local, however, and never more than temporary. The Red tide would soon be in full spate and unstoppable.

It was against this backdrop of change that the role of the *Stukawaffe* began to alter too. Although no longer spearheading spectacular German advances, the Ju 87s would still be called upon to attack targets in the enemy hinterland – mainly bridges, troop concentrations and communications centres – in order to disrupt the Red Army's lines of

A mechanic warms up the engine of a winter-camouflaged Ju 87D-3 on a bleak forward landing ground 'somewhere in Russia'. Just visible are the mainwheel chocks and a bomb on the ground beneath the rudder that is being used as an anchor to weigh down the tail!

The fearsome Tiger tank first went into action on the eastern front at the beginning of 1943. This is a Stuka pilot's eye view of Waffen-SS grenadiers, supported by a Tiger, advancing over ground already cleared by dive-bombing – note the typical pattern of bomb craters staining the snow and still smoking after a recent Stuka attack

reinforcement and supply. But it was over the battlefield itself that the Stukas were being employed with increasing frequency to break up massed Soviet armoured attacks. In effect, Stuka crews were slowly but surely being transformed from 'flying artillery' into 'flying anti-tank gunners'.

So concerned were the Germans about the seemingly limitless numbers of tanks and armoured vehicles being produced by the enemy that the Luftwaffe had been ordered to set up an experimental anti-tank unit (*Versuchskommando für Panzerbekämpfung*) to determine the best way of dealing with the problem. Activated at the Rechlin test centre late in 1942, the unit's task was to evaluate various aircraft/heavy weapon combinations to find the most efficient tank-buster.

After moving to the Bryansk troop training grounds in Russia in the spring of 1943 for field trials, it soon became evident that the *Kommando*'s Ju 87G *Staffeln*, commanded by the experienced Hauptmann Hans-Karl Stepp, offered the best prospects. The G-model was a development of the combat-proven Ju 87D equipped with a 3.7 cm cannon under each wing. Ironically, however, the new weapon system would first demonstrate its formidable capabilities not against tanks, but over water.

Even before the German surrender at Stalingrad, the Red Army had begun to advance across the Don bend on the first lap of its long march to Berlin. The featureless steppe between the Rivers Don and Donets offered little in the way of natural cover, but the area was riven by *balkas*, or small ravines, formed from dried-out water courses. It was ideal tank-busting country, and the *'Doras'* of I./StG 2 were aloft whenever the weather permitted. If the crews were unable to catch any enemy tanks out in the open, they could always be sure of finding some hiding in the *balkas*. 'It was', as one veteran pilot described it, 'a bit like searching for lice in the creases of your undershirt'.

The Germans were desperate to prevent the Soviets from crossing the Donets, for once they did so the enemy would have a clear run along the northern shores of the Sea of Azov towards the Black Sea. This, in turn, would effectively cut off Army Group 'A' down in the Caucasus and precipitate a disaster even greater than Stalingrad.

Army Group 'A' was already disengaging from the Caucasus trap and attempting to get back to the relative safety of the Ukraine. It had three avenues of escape – via the Rostov bottleneck over the Lower Don, across the frozen surface of the Sea of Azov, or up into the Kuban peninsula in the northwest corner of the Caucasus and from there over the narrow Kerch Straits on to the Crimea.

The first of these options disappeared when Rostov was recaptured by the Red Army on 14 February. Shortly afterwards the melting ice on the

The unmistakable silhouette of another newcomer to the front early in 1943 – the 37 mm cannon-armed Ju 87G tank-buster. As feared from the air as the Tiger was on the ground, the *'Gustav'* would remain a potent tank-killer right up until the end of the war

CHAPTER THREE

By the close of January 1943, the 26 machines of Hauptmann Gustav Pressler's III./StG 2 were operating under the control of *Luftwaffenkommando Don*. In this photograph, the *Gruppenkommandeur's* 'AD' is seen shortly after it had been given a fresh coat of winter white overall. But exhaust staining is already beginning to build up again, and the CO's crew chief has not been entirely successful in re-applying the *Geschwader* code – the top bar of the 'T' is decidedly uneven and that '6' is definitely non-standard

Sea of Azov was no longer strong enough to bear the weight of 40. *Panzerkorps'* armoured vehicles. This left just the Kuban. Seizing the opportunity, the Soviets threw everything they had into the fight to prevent Army Group 'A' from establishing a bridgehead across the base of the Kuban peninsula. Equally determined to keep open the one remaining escape route on to the Crimea, the Germans responded in kind.

Among the units rushed down into the area was the experimental anti-tank *Kommando*, and within its ranks was a newcomer. During operations along the Donets front on 10 February, Oberleutnant Hans-Ulrich Rudel had become the first Luftwaffe pilot to fly 1000 operational missions. He had then joined the *Kommando* at Bryansk after a spell of leave, and transferred with it to Kerch, on the eastern tip of the Crimea.

The Ju 87G's baptism of fire against Soviet tanks south of Krimskaya was not an unqualified success. Unable to dive because of the stress imposed by the additional weight of its underwing guns, the

10 February 1943, and celebrations are in full swing at Gorlovka as Oberleutnant Hans-Ulrich Rudel, the *Staffelkapitän* of 1./StG 2, returns from his 1000th operational mission. A laughing Rudel (left) is wearing a label with the words *Hals- und Beinbruch* ('Break your neck and a leg', a traditional term of good luck). His wingman is clutching a lucky pig, and between them is the blacked-up figure of a top-hatted chimney sweep – yet another symbol of good luck. Wearing the flying helmet, a momentarily preoccupied Feldwebel Erwin Hentschel, Rudel's long-time air-gunner, would himself clock up his 1000th mission on 12 August 1943

Kanonenvogel's (cannon-bird's) method of attack was to approach the target at low level. But the growing strength of the enemy's flak defences made this a risky business – as Rudel found to his cost when hit during the unit's first mission. The solution was to provide the Ju 87Gs with an 'escort' of bomb-carrying *'Doras'* to keep the defenders' heads down.

Failing to destroy the bridgehead by direct armoured assault, the Soviets next tried to turn the Kuban front by amphibious landings behind the German lines. The Gulf of Temryuk, on the northern coast of the peninsula, is a maze of lagoons, swamps and interconnecting waterways. It was here that the Russians attempted to infiltrate the best part of two divisions in hundreds of small wooden boats, each carrying from five to twenty men.

This unlikely scenario was the setting for the *Kanonenvogel*'s first major success as they prevented the Soviet forces from landing and consolidating around Temryuk in the German rear. The indefatigable Hans-Ulrich Rudel once more;

'We are in the air every day from dawn until dusk, skimming above the water and the reeds in search of boats. In tackling them we do not need our special tungsten-cored anti-tank ammunition – any high-explosive rounds will suffice to smash the flimsy craft. Normal contact-fused Flak ammunition proves to be the most suitable. Anything we catch trying to cross the open stretches of water is as good as lost. I alone destroy 70 of these vessels in the space of a few days.'

Despite continued Soviet pressure, the Kuban bridgehead would hold out until September. But it was not just in the far south that the Red Army was pushing hard. By early 1943 the Germans were coming under attack all along the eastern front.

In the third week of February a special Stuka combat group was set up to help restore the situation along the Upper Donets, where the Red Army had recaptured the important town of Byelgorod on 9 February and the Waffen-SS had – much to Hitler's fury – abandoned the city of Kharkov, purportedly one of the strongest German bastions in the Ukraine, just seven days later.

The *Führer* ordered that Kharkov be retaken forthwith. And it was to support the ground forces assigned to this task that the *Gefechtsverband* Hozzel was created. It comprised I. and II./StG 2, together with the attached II./StG 1 and I./StG 77, the former fresh from re-equipment at Nikolayev and the latter hastily recalled from a brief stint in the Kuban.

Oddly, the Red Army fielded little armour against the advancing Germans, and for the veterans among the Stuka crews it was quite like old times as they revelled in several days of operations performing their traditional role of 'flying artillery'. Kharkov and Byelgorod were both reoccupied in mid-

With bombs already detonating off to the left, these two Stukas of II./StG 77 (bottom right) are intent on another target. The two black dots immediately above them are Soviet armoured vehicles that have left the convoy on the road in the centre of the picture and are seeking the 'safety' of open fields – according to an accompanying report, neither made it

March. But by that time Major Hozzel's combat group had long been disbanded, as its component *Gruppen* were more urgently required elsewhere. While II./StG 1 was sent northwards to join its parent *Geschwaderstab* on the central sector and I./StG 77 returned to the southern Ukraine, I. and II./StG 2 were transferred further south still to Kerch, on the Crimea, where they were to continue the Luftwaffe's support of the Kuban bridgehead.

It was at Kerch that StG 2 was used to form the nucleus of another temporary dive-bomber battle group. Headed by the *Geschwader's* new *Kommodore*, the *Stukaverband* Kupfer consisted of all three of its *Gruppen*, I./StG 2 flying down to the Crimea in April after having spent the past six months operating primarily along the Upper Don sector around the town of Voronezh.

Also attached to Kupfer's command was II./StG 77, another unit that had recently re-equipped at Nikolayev, and I./StG 3. This last was a new addition to the ranks of the eastern front's Stuka force. A veteran of the North African campaign, I./StG 3 had been pulled out of Libya at the end of 1942 and returned to the Reich for rest and re-equipment. But in February 1943, instead of heading back to the desert, it had been sent to the Kuban, where it took part in the fighting to eliminate the Soviet beachhead established south of the Black Sea port of Novorossisk. After this it joined the *Stukaverband* in the Crimea, where it would remain for the next three months. Having lost its *Kommandeur*, Major Horst Schiller, to anti-aircraft fire northwest of Krimskaya on 2 June, I./StG 3 finally returned to the Mediterranean theatre in July.

It was while at Kerch that the *Staffelkapitän* of 1./StG 2, Hans-Ulrich Rudel, was promoted to Hauptmann (with effect from 1 April, retroactive as of 1 April 1942 for conspicuous bravery in action). The one-time misfit was by now fully established. And even more so a fortnight later when he was awarded the Oak Leaves to his Knight's Cross, the presentation being made by Hitler in person at the Reich's Chancellery in Berlin.

At the beginning of May, the whole of StG 2 was suddenly rushed back up to the Kharkov area, only for I. and III. *Gruppen* to return to the

Still wearing its winter camouflage, a *'Dora'* of I./StG 77 churns through the melting snow of the spring thaw as it lands back at base after a mission

Crimea again a few days later. The Luftwaffe's 'fire brigade' was still functioning smoothly! And in mid-June its firepower was given a substantial boost when one of the experimental anti-tank *Kommando*'s two original Ju 87G *Staffeln*, 2./*Vers.Kdo. für Pz.Bekämpfung*, was officially incorporated into the *Geschwader* as the *Panzerjägerstaffel* (*Pz.J.St.*)/StG 2.

The *Versuchskommando*'s 1. *Staffel* was likewise redesignated on 17 June to become *Pz.J.St.*/StG 1. This *Geschwader* had been fighting hard on the central sector since early February. On 3 March it had been unable to prevent the Red Army from liberating Rzhev, one of the last towns to be taken by the victorious Germans during their advance on Moscow in the autumn of 1941. But the *Führer* was determined that Bryansk and Orel, two towns to the south of Rzhev that had also fallen to his forces in October 1941, should be held at all costs (and for the same reason that he had insisted Kharkov be recaptured after its premature abandonment by the Waffen-SS, as will shortly be made clear).

It has been claimed that a heavy Luftwaffe raid on Livny, the hub of the Red Army's rear-area supply network on the Orel front, was instrumental in bringing the Soviet offensive in this region to a grinding halt. From the back seat of the *'Dora'* flown by Knight's Cross holder Oberleutnant Erwin-Peter Diekwisch of 9./StG 1, a war correspondent described the 13 March raid;

'The Stukas were the first to take off, followed by the fighters and then the He 111s. The machines circled as they got into formation. The front line was crossed at an altitude of 3000 m (10,000 ft). The fighters protected the formation and drove off a Russian fighter attack. After 15 minutes flying time, Livny lay beneath us. Two of our *Staffeln* were ordered to attack the railway station, and the third targeted an area identified as an ammunition depot.

'We raced earthwards, releasing our heavy bombs at 600 m (2000 ft). Three long goods trains standing in the station were hit. They burst into flames and then exploded when the munitions in the wagons went up.

'With a thunderous detonation the ammunition dump also flew into the air. A thick column of black smoke climbed some 1000 m (3500 ft) into the sky.

'Our Stukas recovered and climbed away. As they turned for home, sticks of bombs from the He 111s were already falling across the centre of town, which was packed with Russians troops. Here, too, ammunition was exploding in all directions and fuel dumps were burning. Livny had ceased to exist.'

Not all the *Geschwader*'s missions were as successful as this, however. When bombing another railway station to the south of Orel a few days later, II./StG 1 lost half of its 36-strong attacking force – nine aircraft shot down, and another nine sustaining heavy damage that would require major repairs.

While II. and III./StG 1 were doing their bit towards holding the central sector together, there was only one *Stukagruppe* along the entire 1200 miles (2000 km) of front stretching away to the north of them. But the unit in question, I./StG 5, was no longer ploughing its own lonely furrow far above the Arctic Circle. Late in January its 32 Stukas had been transferred down to the Leningrad sector south of Lake Ladoga. And for

This groundcrewman of II./StG 1 does not seem to know where to start patching. The line of bullet exit holes through the fuselage cross would seem to indicate a fighter attack from the starboard quarter. Note the unusual treatment of the individual letter 'O'

CHAPTER THREE

Soon to undergo further redesignation to become I./StG 1, the machines of I./StG 5 operating on both the Arctic and Leningrad fronts were still wearing the 'L1' codes from their pre-war days as IV.(St)/LG 1. Here, the *Gruppenstab's* 'L1+CB' prepares to take off

the next five months it would divide its strength (a 4. *Staffel* having been created by redesignating the unit's *Ergänzungsstaffel*) and energies between these two areas.

For those elements of the *Gruppe* based south of Leningrad, this meant operating against the Red Army divisions massing along the Volkhov front between Lakes Ladoga and Ilmen. The units in the far north, including 4./StG 5, continued the long-running campaign against the Murmansk railway leading south from Russia's Arctic ports. Between January and June 1943 some 200 separate attacks were mounted against this supply lifeline. These reportedly cost the *Gruppe* just four machines!

Then, early in June, I./StG 5 underwent another redesignation to become I./StG 1. In this guise it transferred to the central sector, where it joined II. and III./StG 1 under its new parent *Stab*. This *Geschwader's* I. *Gruppe* slot had been vacant since the original I./StG 1, then based in North Africa, had been redesignated II./StG 3 in January 1942. And just to complicate matters even further, June also saw the arrival on the central sector of III./StG 3 – the original II./StG 2! – after its withdrawal from Tunisia the previous month.

In order to retain a Stuka presence in the far north, a new I./StG 5 was activated from scratch at Bodö, in Norway, on 17 June. This then took on the traditional roles of the dive-bomber in the Arctic, first attacking the Murmansk railway from its base at Alakurtti before, in August, mounting raids out of Nautsi, south of Petsamo, on Russian ports and harbour installations along the Arctic Ocean coast. But these activities were a sideshow, both geographically and operationally. The last major act in the drama of the Ju 87 dive-bomber on the eastern front was about to begin.

Hitler's insistence on holding Orel and recapturing Kharkov had created two firm 'shoulders', some 235 miles (380 km) apart, astride the boundary between Army Groups Centre and South. Roughly equidistant between Orel and Kharkov, the important railway junction town of Kursk had been taken by the Red Army on 7 February. Since then the Soviets had continued to push westwards, driving a huge fist-like salient, or 'bulge', deep into the German frontline.

This was the setting for the *Führer's* 1943 summer offensive. Code-named Operation *Zitadelle*, its aims were far less grandiose than

The first Ju 87D-5s, armed with 20 mm wing guns, were reportedly delivered to III./StG 2 just prior to Operation *Zitadelle*. 'T6+AS' pictured here may have been the mount of Hauptmann Bernhard Wutka, *Staffelkapitän* of 8./StG 2, who was killed on the fourth day of the Battle of Kursk

Luftwaffe air liaison officers (*Fliegerverbindungsoffiziere*, or '*Flivos*' for short), who were attached to army units in the field to provide direct radio contact with the supporting Stukas, played an important role in the Kursk fighting. Here, a *Flivo* stands in an open-topped armoured command half-track – note the rectangular frame antenna that surrounds him – as a *Kette* of Ju 87D-5s roars low overhead

either *Barbarossa* of 1941 or the twin advances on Stalingrad and the Caucasus in 1942. Hitler's present plans were for his armies to push inwards from the northern and southern shoulders of the salient, join forces, sever it at the base and destroy or capture the Soviet armies trapped within the bulge. Although *Zitadelle's* territorial ambitions were not huge, both sides were well aware of the significance of the coming confrontation, and built up their forces accordingly. Kursk was thus destined to become the largest tank battle in military history.

To support the German ground forces, the Luftwaffe amassed a total of some 1800 aircraft. Over 350 of this number were Stukas. On the northern flank, in the Orel area, were the three *Gruppen* of StG 1, together with the '*Gustavs*' of its anti-tank *Staffel*. To the south, around Kharkov, were gathered all six *Gruppen* of StGs 2 and 77, plus the former's anti-tank *Kanonenvögel*.

Launched on 5 July, the Battle of Kursk is rightly recognised as an historic land engagement. But like all German offensives that preceded it, *Zitadelle* began with a series of pre-emptive air strikes. StG 1's first target was the town of Kursk itself, as Major Friedrich Lang, the *Kommandeur* of III. *Gruppe*, recounts;

'This attack was to open *Zitadelle*. The whole *Geschwader* was taking part, but the first wave was to be flown by my *Gruppe* and the machines of the *Stab*. It began a few minutes after 0400 hrs.

'Our approach flight was not disrupted, despite the fact that our aircraft were plainly visible to the enemy. Only when our machines were circling the town of Kursk did the Russian flak come up to greet us.

'We had reached the southern point of our attack position and were preparing to commence our dive in a northerly direction along the axis of the railway depot before the Russian fighters began taking off from their fields to the east of town. The first Russian attack did not come in until the leading machine was recovering from its dive. The rest of the *Gruppe* was not molested, even though a large number of Russian fighters had got into the air very quickly.

'Our second *Gruppe*, which attacked a few minutes later, suffered heavy losses from these enemy fighter sorties.'

This attack on Kursk railway station was to be the last dive-bomber raid flown by III./StG 1 deep behind enemy lines. Henceforth, not just StG 1 but every Stuka unit in the east would be employed almost exclusively in direct support of ground forces on the battlefield. But the strength of the aerial opposition at Kursk – the Soviets had nearly 3000 frontline aircraft immediately available in the area, including many of their latest Lavochkin La-5 and Yakovlev Yak-9 fighters – meant that the Stuka's classic shortcoming, its inability to survive in hostile airspace, was once again about to be laid bare.

III./StG 1's forward field is a hive of activity as its aircraft are bombed-up in readiness for another mission

With the protective mantle of air superiority stripped from them, the losses among Stuka crews began to increase alarmingly. July 1943 was to be the costliest month of all for the eastern front *Stukagruppen*. Their casualty lists included many experienced and irreplaceable unit leaders.

Although III./StG 1's machines had all returned safely from the opening strike on Kursk railway station, the *Gruppe* lost three aircraft later that same day. Among the casualties were Oberleutnant Hermann Rohde, the *Kapitän* of 9. *Staffel*, and his air-gunner, who were both injured when their Stuka overturned while making an emergency landing after being hit by anti-aircraft fire.

On 8 July the two southern *Stukageschwader* each suffered the loss of a *Staffelkapitän* and a Knight's Cross holder when the machines of Hauptleute Bernhard Wutka and Karl Fitzner, of 8./StG 2 and 5./StG 77 respectively, both exploded in mid-air during attacks on enemy tanks.

Zitadelle soon began to run into difficulties. Despite almost superhuman efforts by ground and air forces alike, little progress was being made from either the northern or southern shoulders of the salient. Then, on 12 July, a powerful Russian counter-offensive aimed at Orel threatened to encircle and cut off all the German troops ranged along the northern edge of the bulge. This, and the Anglo-American landings in Sicily 48 hours earlier (which necessitated a large-scale redeployment of forces from the eastern front to the hitherto thinly-held 'soft underbelly of Europe') convinced Hitler on 13 July to call a halt to *Zitadelle*.

This did not save Oberleutnant Günther Schmid, the *Kapitän* of 5./StG 2, who was shot down northeast of Byelgorod the following day. And on 17 July, the date on which the German disengagement from the Kursk salient got underway, no fewer than three commanders were lost. By this stage StG 2 had already been transferred from the southern to the northern shoulder of the salient to help counter the Russian threat developing to the rear of 9. *Armee*, and it was here in the Orel area that all three casualties occurred.

Hauptmann Friedrich Lorenz, the *Staffelkapitän* of 1./StG 1 – a veteran of the Arctic front during the days of IV.(St.)/LG 1 and I./StG 5 – was another whose Stuka exploded in mid-air. He had just started his dive when an anti-aircraft shell struck the bomb his machine was carrying and it disintegrated, killing both crewmembers instantly.

By contrast, Oberleutnant Egbert Jaekel, the *Staffelkapitän* of 2./StG 2, had been engaged on the main sectors of the eastern front since the very start of *Barbarossa*. He had claimed a direct hit on a cruiser

'T6+AC' of *Stab* II./StG 2 was left riddled with bomb fragment splinters after a Red Air Force raid on the *Gruppe's* base at Karachev, near Orel

Visible in the cockpit of the nearest machine (a Ju 87D-5 bearing the green spinner tip of a *Gruppenstab* aircraft) is Hauptmann Hans-Ulrich Rudel, the recently appointed *Kommandeur* of III./StG 2, who is preparing to lead one of his *Staffeln* out for a massed take-off sometime in the early autumn of 1943

during StG 2's attacks on the Soviet fleet at Kronstadt in September 1941. But as a Stuka pilot his unlikely, possibly unique, specialty was his willingness and ability to take on Russian fighters. He always contended that his machine was particularly fast, and that at full throttle it could leave all the others in the *Gruppe* standing. It is said that he already had close on a dozen enemy fighters to his credit, and that he never hesitated to tackle any he encountered.

His 983rd mission, flown on the morning of 17 July, was to be no different. The Stukas of I./StG 2 were just returning back across their own lines after having dive-bombed a nearby Red Army artillery battery when somebody reported a gaggle of Russian fighters. The enemy aeroplanes were some distance away, and showing no signs of attacking, but Jaekel immediately turned towards them. He shot down one of the La-5s, but another – which his equally belligerent back seat air-gunner, Oberfeldwebel Fritz 'Tubby' Jentzsch, apparently failed to spot – quickly got on his tail. Hit at an altitude of only 650 ft (200 m), neither Jaekel nor Jentzsch managed to escape from the mortally wounded *'Dora'* which crashed and exploded in flames on impact.

III./StG 2 had already lost its *Gruppenkommandeur* in the early hours of that same 17 July when Major Walter Krauss was killed by bomb fragments during the latest of the nightly harassment raids that the *Gruppe* had been subjected to since arriving at Orel-East. Krauss had been the first reconnaissance pilot to be awarded the Knight's Cross (in July 1940) for his exploits during the Battle of France) before transferring to the Stuka arm in the winter of 1941-42. He had received his dive-bomber training with Rudel's *Ergänzungsstaffel* at Graz, in Austria. And it was

Hauptmann Hans-Ulrich Rudel who now took Krauss' place at the head of III./StG 2.

The German retreat from the Kursk salient brought no respite. Quite the reverse. The Soviets were increasing their pressure all along the line, and German forces had to fall back even further. Towns which had been in their hands for two years or more were now being retaken by the advancing Red Army one after the other. And the ten eastern front *Stukagruppen*, whose serviceable strength in the aftermath of *Zitadelle* numbered just 184 machines in total – well below 50 per cent of establishment – could do very little to prevent it.

Of those *Gruppen* that had been engaged on the northern flank of the Kursk bulge, II./StG 1 was deployed briefly to the Leningrad area at the end of July, before returning to the central sector early the following month. There, the Red Army had taken Orel on 5 August and II./StG 1 rejoined its parent *Stab* in the general retreat north-westwards towards Smolensk. By mid-September StG 1 was based around Shatalovka, only some 35 miles (55 km) south of the town. But 9. *Armee,* which had successfully extricated itself from Orel, withdrew from Smolensk on 24 September upon the approach of the Red Army. StG 1 was forced to alter course. After detaching a dozen crews to Orsha to undergo nightflying training, the rest of the *Geschwader* headed south-westwards early in October towards Bobruisk, a town that would not fall until the great Soviet summer offensive of 1944.

Having been rushed to the northern shoulder of the Kursk salient to help counter the Russian threat to Orel, the Stukas of StG 2 were also

On 9 October 1943, Hans-Ulrich Rudel was again being photographed (for a wartime propaganda magazine) with a lucky piglet – this time at Bolshaya-Kostromka on the occasion of his 1500th operational mission . . .

. . . and when Hauptmann Rudel went to Hitler's 'Wolf's Lair' HQ in East Prussia on 25 November to receive the Swords to his Oak Leaves, he insisted that his air-gunner, Oberfeldwebel Erwin Hentschel, who had long been nominated for a Knight's Cross, should come along as well – even though it was no longer customary for the *Führer* to present the Knight's Cross in person. An exception was obviously made in the case of the Luftwaffe's most successful air-gunner, for he is seen here in the background standing stiffly to attention and awaiting his turn as Rudel receives his Swords from Hitler. The Oberstleutnant on the left, incidentally, is Dietrich Hrabak, *Geschwaderkommodore* of JG 52, who has just been awarded the Oak Leaves for his 118 aerial victories

Meanwhile, back at Bolshaya-Kostromka in October, another celebration had taken place. A much more muted affair, it marked the 900th operational mission of Rudel's fellow-*Gruppenkommandeur*, Hauptmann Dr Maximilian Otte of II./StG 2, and involved the presentation not of a lucky piglet, but a wooden rocking-horse! Seen at bottom left, it was presumably intended as a gift for the good doctor's offspring

initially caught up in the retreat towards Smolensk following the cancellation of *Zitadelle*. But, staging via Karachev, they had only retired as far as Bryansk before being urgently summoned southwards again. On 5 August – the day Orel was taken – the Soviets captured Byelgorod and advanced on Kharkov. StG 2 was deployed on airfields in and around the city, but could not prevent it finally being taken by the Red Army on 23 August. And this time it would stay in Russian hands.

The whole area to the south of Kharkov, along the Rivers Donets and Mius down to Taganrog, on the Sea of Azov, was highly vulnerable to Soviet attack and could not be held for long. The crews of StG 2 spent September covering the troops of 8. and 1. *Panzerarmeen* as they fell back on the next great water barrier, the River Dnepr. By the last week of the month they were operating out of Dnepropetrovsk on the eastern bank of the river. But incessant enemy air attacks made the field untenable, and on 28 September they withdrew yet further to a landing ground close to the industrial city of Krivoi Rog, some 60 miles (96 km) behind the Dnepr defence line.

On 9 October the airstrip at Kostromka was the scene of rare celebration when Hauptmann Hans-Ulrich Rudel became the first pilot to fly 1500 operational sorties. That morning's attack on Soviet armour approaching Zaporozhye was also the 1200th mission for Rudel's long-time air-gunner, Oberfeldwebel Erwin Hentschel. In addition to the obligatory garlands, lucky piglet and bottles of champagne, the occasion even prompted a visit from *General der Flieger* Kurt Pflugbeil. Nor did the GOC IV. *Fliegerkorps* come empty handed. Knowing that the famously teetotal *Gruppenkommandeur* of III./StG 2 was also the possessor of an extremely sweet tooth, the General brought with him a very large cake!

But individual achievements, however impressive, were the proverbial drop in the ocean, and could do no more than cause temporary local disruptions in the Red Army's flood-tide advance westwards. StG 2's companion *Geschwader* on the southern sector, StG 77, was likewise fully engaged in supporting German ground units as they withdrew from the Donets-Mius positions back to the line of the Dnepr.

On the left-hand flank, I./StG 77 fell back from Kharkov via Krasnograd and Poltava. On the right, II. and III. *Gruppen* retreated to Stalino and along the northern shore of the Sea of Azov, through Mariupol and Melitopol, towards the Crimea. It was one of the latter units that scored what was arguably the *Stukawaffe's* last significant success in the east. And, fittingly perhaps, it was against their adversaries of old – the warships of the Soviet Black Sea Fleet.

During the night of 5/6 October, a group of Russian destroyers bombarded German evacuation ports and shipping along the southern coast of the Crimea. *Kharkov*, the flotilla leader, shelled Yalta, while her

CHAPTER THREE

Minus wheel-spats and a distinctive *Staffel* badge, and displaying the *Geschwader's* 'S7' fuselage code in its reduced size, 7./StG 77's 'ER' patrols the Black Sea coast

Times were getting hard. When Feldwebel Friedrich Maahs, an air-gunner with I./StG 77, who had been awarded the German Cross in Gold back in May 1943, clocked up his 700th operational mission later in the year, there was no longer any greenery to be had. His 'garland' was a mainwheel inner tube!

two smaller consorts were ordered to target Feodosia. But the pair ran into five E-boats and became engaged instead in a sharp, but inconclusive, skirmish some miles off the coast. Before dawn the three Soviet vessels had rendezvoused and were heading back out to sea. They were spotted at first light by a Luftwaffe reconnaissance aircraft.

Alerted by radio, Stukas of StG 77 were despatched to find them. In their first attack the dive-bombers concentrated on the 2500-ton *Kharkov*, which received several hits and was left motionless in the water. She was taken in tow by the *Sposobny*. The second wave of Stukas split into three, hoping to confuse the ships' anti-aircraft gunners as they attacked all three vessels simultaneously.

The *Kharkov* received further severe damage. The *Bezposhchadny* was also badly hit. Less seriously damaged, the *Sposobny* now began heroic efforts to tow the other two destroyers alternatively in a desperate attempt to get them out of range of the Stukas. But it was a hopeless task. The next attack by StG 77 found the *Bezposhchadny* lying dead in the water. A direct hit must have touched off her magazines, for she blew apart in a tremendous explosion. A little later the *Kharkov* was struck again. As she started to founder the captain ordered his crew to abandon ship.

The fourth and final assault by the Stukas of StG 77 found the damaged *Sposobny* picking up survivors from her two sister vessels. After two direct hits she too sank. Informed of the loss of three modern destroyers, Stalin promptly ordered that no large Soviet warship – from destroyers upwards – was to put to sea without his express permission.

The crews of StG 77 had proved beyond a doubt that the Stuka dive-bomber was still a weapon to be reckoned with against ships at sea – even fast and manoeuvrable destroyers – provided they had no air cover. But on land it was a different story. The dive-bomber was no longer the most effective way available of dealing with the masses of Soviet armour that dominated every battlefield. Moreover, it was becoming increasingly vulnerable to the newer generations of Red Air Force fighters.

The Luftwaffe High Command recognised that the way ahead lay with the dedicated *Schlacht*, or ground-attack, aircraft. Consisting of just a single *Gruppe* of obsolescent biplanes at the beginning of the war, the *Schlacht* arm was, by the autumn of 1943, developing into a formidable force equipped primarily with Fw 190 fighter-bombers.

Although transformed from *Stukageschwader* into *Schlachtgeschwader* in October 1943, it was still business as usual for most Ju 87 units for many months to come. The first light dusting of winter snow has already fallen as this unidentified Ju 87D-5 prepares for take-off with a full weapon load. Note the hefty *Dinortstab* on the 250-kg (550-lb) underwing bomb

The Focke-Wulf was a tough, well-armoured machine ideally suited to the job. And once it had delivered its weapon load, it did not have to run for home – as was the Stuka's usual practice – but could stay close to the scene of action and mix it with Soviet fighters on more or less equal terms (in the highest scoring Fw 190 *Schlacht* a pilot was credited with a staggering 116 aerial victories).

The parallel, even if fundamentally different, ground support roles performed by the Stuka and *Schlacht* units made a strong case for their being amalgamated into one arm. There were those who believed that the *Schlachtgruppen* should be assimilated into the still numerically superior *Stukawaffe* to provide a much-needed injection of fresh blood. In the event, the opposite happened. On 18 October the Stuka units – many with histories dating back to the mid-1930s – were redesignated to become part of a greatly enlarged ground-attack arm. Henceforth StGs 1, 2, 3, 5 and 77 would all be referred to as *Schlachtgeschwader*.

At the stroke of a pen the Luftwaffe's infamous dive-bombers – on paper at least – had ceased to exist!

Almost symbolic in its simplicity, a classic shot of a winter-dappled 'Dora' of StG 2 setting out on yet another mission to try to stop the tide of Soviet armour from flooding westwards across that flat, frozen, landscape far below

CHAPTER FOUR

1941-45 – ALLIES COME AND ALLIES GO

One fact often overlooked, or simply ignored, is that the German Wehrmacht was not alone in its campaign against the Soviet Union. The Luftwaffe, for example, enjoyed – on some occasions tolerated would perhaps be a more accurate description – the support of a number of Axis satellite air forces. Five other nations flew the Ju 87 Stuka on the eastern front, and for the sake of completeness, brief details of each are given below.

Rumania

The largest foreign operator of the Stuka in the east, Rumania had asked Germany for 60 Ju 87Bs as early as 1939, but this request was turned down. Even after the launch of *Barbarossa* in June 1941, Hitler was reluctant to supply his Rumanian allies with modern combat aircraft, encouraging them instead to build up their homeland anti-aircraft defences in order to protect the Ploesti region which supplied him with much of his oil.

It was 18 months into the Russian campaign before the Rumanians tried again. One of their bomber groups, which had been operating a mix of Rumanian, Polish and French machines on the Stalingrad front, was

Included in the first batch of Ju 87Ds supplied to Rumania, this machine's Luftwaffe origins are readily apparent from the crudely overpainted swastika on its tail. A small number '10' (its *Grupul* 3 identity) has been chalked on the dark rectangle, and this marking is repeated more clearly on the rudder alongside it

pulled out of the line in December 1942. Wanting to convert *Grupul* 3 into a dive-bomber unit, the Rumanians approached Germany for a delivery of Ju 87s. This time the *Führer* was more amenable, but anxious to keep control of the Stukas in his own hands, he stipulated that the machines were not be sold to Rumania outright, but supplied on loan from Luftwaffe stocks.

In the spring of 1943 the first of an initial batch of 45 Ju 87Ds was flown to Nikolayev, where the Rumanian crews were to be trained on their new mounts. Among the German instructors was Leutnant Anton Andorfer, one of I./StG 77's most experienced and successful pilots. Despite some reservations as to their operational readiness, the Rumanians were transferred forward to Mariupol-West, on the shores of the Sea of Azov, in mid-June.

Grupul 3 flew its first mission as a Stuka unit on 17 June 1943, attacking two villages occupied by Soviet troops. All ten machines returned safely, but the following day the Rumanians suffered their first casualty when a *'Dora'*, damaged by enemy anti-aircraft fire, crashed on return to Mariupol. For the next two weeks the *Grupul* operated daily over the River Mius front without losing a single aircraft. Then, on 5 July, it was ordered down to Bagerovo (Kerch VI) on the eastern tip of the Crimea.

From here, while *Zitadelle* raged to the north of it, *Grupul* 3 provided the only Axis bomber support for the German and Rumanian forces holding the Kuban bridgehead on the far side of the Kerch Straits. On its first operation over the Kuban – flown on 6 July by nine aircraft led by Leutnant Andorfer, now *Grupul* 3's liaison officer – two Stukas were lost. Despite this unpromising start, the *Grupul* quickly proved itself, not only supporting the ground troops, but also laying mines and attacking small Soviet naval vessels off the coast. Its performance while at Kerch VI has been described as 'probably the best direct support the German army ever received from another Axis force during the war'.

But it came at a cost. Originally told it would only be on the Crimea for 20 days at the most (presumably in the expectation of a swift German victory at Kursk), *Grupul* 3 would, in fact, remain there for nearly three months. By the end of the first four weeks, 33 of its 45 aircraft had sustained damage of one sort or another. By the time it left Bagerovo on 1 October, nine machines in all had been lost.

But after just a fortnight in the southern Ukraine, where the Red Army was now advancing westwards along the Sea of Azov from Mariupol towards Melitopol, *Grupul* 3 found itself back on the Crimea, this time based at Karankut, in the northern half of the peninsula. It was to stay here for the next six months, helping to defend the Crimea against constant Soviet pressure from two sides. To the north, land access to the Ukraine was cut off when the Russians reached and sealed the Perekop Isthmus early in November. By that time the Kuban bridge-

Nelly looks much more purposeful – not to say downright war-weary – with her wheel-spats removed. *Grupul* 3 operated two number '15s', the first one being damaged beyond repair late in July 1943. This is more likely to have been the second, which was written-off the following winter during the unit's final months in the Crimea

head had been evacuated and the Soviets were poised to invade the eastern Crimea across the Kerch Straits.

During its six months at Karankut, *Grupul* 3 flew nearly 1500 individual sorties, losing just 15 aircraft from all causes in the process. All the more galling then, when the time came to evacuate the Crimea, was the order prohibiting the crews from flying out in their own machines. Instead, on 10 April 1944, they were instructed to ferry their Stukas down to Cherson, near Sevastopol, where they were to be handed back to the Luftwaffe (only – according to one report – for them then to be promptly blown up before their eyes).

Transported across the Black Sea to Rumania's main seaplane base at Mamaia by Luftwaffe flying-boat, *Grupul* 3's aircrews were reunited with their ground staff at Tecuci on 14 April. From here a number of pilots were despatched to the Protectorate to collect new aircraft. One of their first missions over their own homeland was an attack by eight machines on a bridge ahead of the advancing Red Army flown on 14 May (Russian forces had crossed the River Prut, the pre-war frontier between Rumania and the Soviet Union, just 12 days earlier).

Meanwhile, a second Rumanian dive-bomber unit, *Grupul* 6, was working up at Krosno, in Poland. By 20 May it had taken up residence at Husi, adding its 28 *'Doras'* to the 25 of *Grupul* 3 at Recuci, some 60 miles (100 km) to the southwest. The two units were soon operating together. On 30 May they mounted a combined total of 93 sorties, losing four aircraft, all but one from the new *Grupul* 6. The next day 69 Stukas attacked enemy armour and artillery emplacements.

The high level of activity continued throughout the first week of June, after which a lull descended on the area. But this was very much the calm before the storm, as the Soviet Army Group South Ukraine was gathering its strength for a major offensive against Rumania. Late in June *Grupul* 3 left the overcrowded field at Tecuci for Carlomanesti, where operations began to pick up again the following month. But then in mid-August, reflecting current Luftwaffe policy of completely re-equipping its erstwhile Stuka arm, the pilots of *Grupul* 3 were ordered to leave their Ju 87s and proceed to Lugoj for retraining on Fw 190 ground-attack aircraft.

The Rumanians were still waiting for the promised Focke-Wulfs when the Soviet offensive began. *Grupul* 6 lost one Stuka on 20 August, the opening day of the Red Army's assault. Hastily recalled from Lugoj to Husi, *Grupul* 3's pilots were in action dive-bombing and strafing Soviet columns two days later. But the enemy's strength was overwhelming. The Rumanians agreed to a cease-fire, which came into effect at 2300 hrs on 23 August. The following morning Luftwaffe personnel seized *Grupul* 6's aircraft,

Also pictured in the Crimea – possibly at Karankut, although one flat expanse of airfield looks very like any other – *Hai Acasa!'s' Grupul* **number is unfortunately not recorded**

which they themselves then manned to fly reprisal raids on the Rumanian capital of Bucharest.

Having escaped the clutches of the Luftwaffe, the crews of *Grupul* 3 suddenly found themselves fighting alongside the Russians when the new Rumanian government declared war against Germany on 25 August. One of their first missions under the new regime was flown on 28 August when they were despatched to attack German barges on the River Danube. But a shortage of spares for the Ju 87Ds soon became a problem, and the following month the two units were combined to form *Grupul 3/6*. Perhaps not surprisingly, most of the aircrews of the new *Grupul* were those ex-members of the relatively fledgling and 'untainted' *Grupul* 6 who had managed to evade German capture – the Soviet authorities were no doubt all too well aware that the veterans of *Grupul* 3 had been fighting the Red Army tooth and nail for well over a year!

Under the control of the 5th Soviet Air Force, Rumanian Stukas would see further limited action over the southern Carpathians against the retreating Germans and Hungarians (Rumania had officially opened hostilities against Hungary on 6 September). But the spares situation continued to plague operations, and by early 1945 the last of *Grupul* 3/6's three component squadrons had been amalgamated with a single squadron of Henschel Hs 129s. By war's end just nine Ju 87Ds remained on strength.

Hungary

Like the Rumanians, Hungary had also made overtures to Germany for a supply of Stukas during the opening months of the war, requesting 'at least' 20 Ju 87Bs in 1940. Unlike Rumania, however, Hungary's approach was not rejected out of hand, but no firm delivery date was given. In the event, it was not until the winter of 1941-42 that the first machines were forthcoming. And this initial batch (reportedly comprising just four obsolete Ju 87As, plus a couple of repaired and

When Hungary received its first Ju 87s they were painted in a two-tone camouflage scheme and carried pre-March 1942 triangular national markings (see Profile 27). But this trio of unarmed *'Berta'* trainers appear to be in standard Luftwaffe finish and are wearing full-chord tail stripes

renovated Bs) was to be used for training purposes only. A further eight *'Bertas'* were delivered some time later.

And there the matter rested for nearly a year. An order for 26 Ju 87s placed with Junkers early in 1940 was abruptly cancelled in May 1942. This may have had something to do with the unreasonably low opinion Hitler had developed of the Hungarians' prowess in the air. When faced with a request from Hungary for yet more Messerschmitt fighters, the *Führer* had scathingly replied;

'The Hungarians' performance to date has been more than poor. If I'm to part with aircraft, then I'd rather they went to the Croats, as they've at least proved they know how to attack. With the Hungarians all we've had so far are fiascos.'

It was not until two Hungarian bomber squadrons equipped with Italian Caproni Ca 135s were withdrawn from the eastern front in September 1942 that Stuka training began in earnest. For while one of these squadron was to re-equip with Ju 88s, the other was ordered to convert to Ju 87s.

Early in 1943 the first of 13 *'Doras'* were finally delivered to Hungary. These were used to form the 12-aircraft strong 102/2 Dive-bomber Squadron. The unit's ground staff set off by road for Kiev, in the southern sector of the Russian front, at the end of May. After several weeks of working up, the squadron transferred briefly to the central sector, where, on 3 August 1943, the crews flew their first operational mission against a large partisan encampment in the forests near Bryansk.

Immediately thereafter 102/2 returned south to Poltava. Here, it was placed under the tactical command of II./StG 77. For almost the next three months the squadron operated in conjunction with Hauptmann Helmut Leicht's *Stukagruppe* as it supported the ground troops in their fight for, and subsequent retreat from, the city of Kharkov. By 8 October 102/2's crews had completed 1000 sorties. An additional 200+ would be flown before they were ordered back to Hungary a fortnight later. During its time at the front 102/2 Dive-bomber Squadron had dropped more than 800 tons (810,000 kg) of bombs. It had also claimed three Soviet fighters shot down – two La-5s and a P-39 Airacobra.

Operational *'Doras'* of the Hungarian air force's 102/2 Dive-bomber Squadron (102/2.Zuhanóbombázö század) over the southern sector in the early autumn of 1943. Note the two styles of tail tricolour striping

But these operations had cost the unit dearly. Historic references differ as to its exact losses, some stating that eight of its original twelve *'Doras'* were shot down, all by enemy anti-aircraft fire. Other sources refer to 15 out of 21 aircraft (presumably including replacements) and six crews being lost.

Whatever the true figures, it appears that the remaining machines were reclaimed by the Luftwaffe, while the squadron personnel returned to Kolozsvár, in Hungary, to train new crews and rebuild the unit. For this purpose Junkers supplied them with ten overhauled *'Bertas'* (although whether these Stukas were the ten originally delivered in 1941-42 and now refurbished or an altogether separate second batch is not clear).

Training commenced in March 1944 – the month of the bloodless occupation of Hungary by German forces and the replacement of the country's wavering regime by a new pro-Nazi government. In May, 12 Ju 87D-5s (out of a promised delivery of 20) arrived at Kolozsvár to enable the crews to complete their operational training. And on 16 June the unit, now apparently officially renumbered as 2/2 Dive-bomber Squadron – although appearing on the Luftwaffe's orders of battle, somewhat confusingly, as the *ung.S.St.* 102/1 (Hungarian *Schlacht Staffel* 102/1) – transferred to III./SG 77's base at Kuniow, in Poland, for final working up.

This move put the squadron directly in the path of the massive Soviet summer offensive of 1944, which would lead to the collapse of Army Group Centre and lay open the way to Berlin. The Hungarians did not fly their first mission until the last day of June, exactly a week after the Red Army launched its assault. In July they retired to Krosno, where I./SG 77 was undergoing conversion from the Ju 87 onto the Fw 190. During July and August, operating out of Krosno, Hordynia and Starzawa, they mounted close on 50 operations against the advancing Soviets, losing five of their twelve aircraft for their pains.

In September the squadron moved back south into its homeland. And on the afternoon of 12 October most of its remaining *'Doras'* were destroyed on the ground at Börgönd during a low-level sweep by Italian-based P-51s of the American Fifteenth Air Force. This effectively wrote finis to the story of the Hungarian Stukas, although a few small-scale attacks on Soviet armoured columns were reportedly carried out during the winter months of 1944/45. Even as late as April 1945 moves were afoot to set up a Hungarian anti-tank squadron equipped with Ju 87Gs, but neither time nor aircraft were available in sufficient quantity to permit this to happen.

Bulgaria

Despite receiving nearly 50 Stukas from a 'sympathetic' Hitler, Bulgaria never used them against the Red Army. In fact, although it signed adhesion to the Axis Pact on 1 March 1941 and allowed German troops onto its soil – and was even persuaded to declare war on Great Britain and the United States on 12 December of that year – Bulgaria's ruler, King Boris, successfully resisted all German demands that he go to war against the much closer Soviet Union.

During the latter half of 1941, 15 Bulgarian pilots did, however, undergo dive-bomber training at the Luftwaffe's Stuka schools at Bad

Aibling and Wertheim. Upon completion of their course, they were transferred to Italy to gain operational experience. The Bulgarian High Command refused permission to let them fly in action against Allied ships in the Mediterranean, however, and they instead returned to their homeland, where they formed the nucleus of the 2nd 'Storm' (i.e. Ground-attack) Regiment activated at Count Ignatievo airfield and equipped with Polish-built PZL P.43B Karas light bomber.

It was to be another two years before the Bulgarian Air Force received its first Stukas in the form of a dozen ex-Luftwaffe Ju 87Rs, an initial batch of six being delivered on 13 August 1943 and the remainder on 6 September. These machines served primarily as trainers.

Five months later, in January-February 1944, Hitler supplied the Bulgarians with 32 *'Doras'*. These were then used to equip the 1st Squadron of the 2nd 'Storm' Regiment, which, during the summer of 1944, operated primarily against partisan units and strongholds in both their own country and neighbouring Yugoslavia.

On 26 August Bulgaria announced its unilateral 'withdrawal from the war'. But its self-declared neutrality did not last long. The Red Army was already at the country's borders, and on 5 September the Soviet Union declared war on Bulgaria – three armies of the 3rd Ukrainian Front crossed the frontier that same day. Bulgarian troops offered no resistance, and on 8 September a newly installed pro-Soviet regime in turn declared war on Germany.

Bulgaria's armed forces soon found themselves fighting alongside the Russians. Their numbers included the 21 serviceable Ju 87Ds of the 2nd 'Storm' Regiment, once the Regiment's CO had been liquidated *'pour encourager les autres'*. Thus the only frontline operations ever undertaken by Bulgarian Stukas were the few ground-attack sorties reportedly flown against their former allies as Axis troops withdrew from Yugoslavia at the end of 1944.

Slovakia

Despite two tours of duty on the eastern front – the first in support of its own ground troops during the opening months of *Barbarossa*, and the second primarily in an anti-partisan capacity from June 1942 until August 1943 – the tiny Slovakian Air Force had as yet received no Stukas from its German benefactors.

It was not until the Soviet spring offensive of 1944 brought the Red Army close to the foot of the Carpathian Mountains guarding Slovakia's eastern borders that two former homeland defence fighter squadrons, Nos 11 and 12, were ordered to begin converting onto Ju 87Ds. The first three *'Doras'* to be delivered, however, were purportedly used to form a mixed squadron, along with a trio of indigenous Letov light bombers, that flew a number of ground-attack missions out of Spisská Nová Ves against the advancing Russians.

'White 46' was one of 32 *'Doras'* supplied to Bulgaria. It is seen here presumably in the markings of the 2nd Storm Regiment's 1st Squadron circa summer 1944

Believed to be the third (see small numeral at base of rudder) of the initial trio of Ju 87Ds received by Slovakia, the fuselage lettering worn here (OK-XAC) may well have been the machine's quasi-civilian delivery markings

But by June 1944 No 11 Squadron had 12 Stukas on strength, five apparently being new D-5s and the rest a mix of Bs and Ds, some of them unarmed and presumably intended for training. And in August the Junkers works recorded the despatch of 11 more refurbished Stukas to Slovakia. Just what became of these machines is not clear, for on 28 August there was a national uprising in Slovakia and the bulk of the regular armed forces promptly sided with the insurgents.

Germany retaliated at once, entering the country from the west. Fierce fighting ensued, but large areas remained under the control of the Slovakian nationalists, and guerrilla warfare continued until the arrival of the Red Army early in 1945. A number of different types of aircraft were gathered together at Tri Duby airfield to form the insurgent 'Combined Squadron', which went into action against the invading Germans. Whether as part of this unit or not, a handful of *'Doras'* are known to have operated in support of the uprising – although at times only one machine was serviceable, which would then apparently be sent out on its own to bomb and strafe German columns!

Of the 24+ Stukas reportedly supplied to Slovakia during 1944, a least one survived into the post-war era.

Croatia

Given the *Führer's* expressed admiration for the Croats' aggressiveness in the air (see page 82), their country seems to have come a surprisingly poor fifth, and last, in the Axis satellite Stuka allocation stakes.

Although semi-autonomous Croatian fighter and bomber squadrons had long been operating under Luftwaffe control on the eastern front, it was the winter of 1943/44 before men and machines of the two Do 17-equipped bomber squadrons were used to form the nucleus of a new group activated at Lucko, in Croatia. This unit was provided with additional Dorniers, half-a-dozen Italian bombers for training purposes and, in the early spring of 1944, three Ju 87R Stukas for anti-partisan operations.

In July, a further 12 R-2s were added to the original trio to create a separate Stuka squadron. And two months later the unit – now listed on the Luftwaffe's order of battle as *1.kr.S.St* (1st Croatian Ground-attack Squadron) – was transferred up to Eichwalde, in East Prussia to commence operations under *Luftflotte* 6.

Details of its subsequent activities are understandably sketchy. In October the Red Army stormed the frontiers of East Prussia, and by the middle of the month *1.kr.S.St* reported all but four of its fourteen machines unserviceable. Early in November the squadron withdrew to Lubenwalde, where it would be ordered to relinquish its remaining aircraft to the Luftwaffe's 1. *Fliegerdivision* before the month was out, thereby bringing to a premature end Croatia's brief operational flirtation with the Ju 87 Stuka.

CHAPTER FIVE

1943-45 – *PANZER-BUSTING POSTSCRIPT*

When the Luftwaffe's *Stukageschwader* were transformed into *Schlachtgeschwader* in October 1943, it was clearly impossible for all the Ju 87s then in service – exactly 275 on the eastern front alone – to be replaced by Fw 190s overnight. Conversion from one type to the other was a process that would extend over many months. Three *Gruppen* were still flying their *'Doras'* over a year later, and one – III./SG 2 – had only just begun re-equipping when the war ended. For a list giving full details of all unit redesignations from Stuka to *Schlacht*, plus their subsequent re-equipment, see *Osprey Aviation Elite Units 13 – Luftwaffe Schlachtgruppen*.

But there was one unit which escaped the wholesale redesignations of 18 October 1943, and that was II. *Gruppe* of StG 2, which simply had the anti-tank suffix (Pz) attached to its title and continued thereafter to operate as II./StG 2(Pz). It is not altogether certain whether the unit remained under the tactical command of its erstwhile parent *Geschwader* (the now SG 2, which had already been provided with a 'new' II. *Gruppe* by the simple expedient of redesignating the three Fw 190-equipped *Staffeln* of the original ground-attack II./SchlG 1). Nor do official records make absolutely clear whether II./StG 2(Pz) was equipped entirely with cannon-armoured Ju 87G tank-busters from the outset.

What is evident, however, is that II./StG 2(Pz) was immediately thrown into action against the Soviet tank armies that had just smashed their way through the Dnepr Line and were now advancing into the western Ukraine. The figures alone tell the story. Two days after adopting its new designation, II./StG 2(Pz) had 24 Stukas on strength, 22 of which were serviceable. By 10 November the corresponding totals had fallen to just nine and eight!

Despite such grievous losses the *Gruppe* continued to mount its attacks on the enemy's armoured spearheads throughout the winter of 1943/44. And on 29 February 1944 one of its members became the last officially designated Stuka pilot to win the Knight's Cross on the eastern front (although many

Soldiering on – a Ju 87G tank-buster of an unidentified *Staffel* pictured during the winter of 1944–45

As the conflict neared its end, even some *'Gustavs'* were being forced to hunt by night. Note the flame-damper exhaust shroud on this cannon-armed Ju 87G, and also the yellow band around the machine's cowling – a recognition marking applied to most Luftwaffe aircraft operating over Hungary at this late stage

more such awards would go to Ju 87 flyers – including ten air-gunners – operating under the *Schlacht* banner between November 1943 and April 1945) when 6. *Staffel's* Oberfeldwebel Jakob Jenster was decorated for completing more than 700 missions.

But after five months as the only *Stukagruppe* on the Luftwaffe's roster, II./StG 2(Pz)'s unique position was about to come to an end. In March 1944 its 6. *Staffel* was disbanded and 4. and 5./StG 2(Pz) were redesignated to become 10.(Pz)/SG 3 and 10.(Pz)/SG 77 respectively. And for much of the last 12 months of the war in Europe, as the remaining *'Dora'*-equipped *Schlachtgruppen* slowly but surely converted to Fw 190s, the only constant Ju 87 presence on the eastern front was provided by the *'Gustavs'* of the four specialised anti-tank *Staffeln*.

In January 1945, however, even their numbers were halved when two of the *Staffeln* underwent further redesignation to become part of the newly activated I.(Pz)/SG 9, with one re-equipping with Fw 190s and the other subsequently being transferred north up into Scandinavia.

And so the story of the Junkers Ju 87's daylight war against the Soviet Union came to a close. It had begun just under four years earlier with eight *Stukagruppen* – nearly 300 machines in all – dominating the skies and demoralising the Red Army in their role as the Wehrmacht's 'flying artillery'. It ended with just two *Staffeln* – 10.(Pz)/SG 2 and 10.(Pz)/SG 77, together fielding a total of some 30 serviceable aircraft – still trying to stop the unstoppable tide of Soviet armour right up until the final day of hostilities in the east.

On 8 May 1945 Leutnant Anton Korol (left), the *Staffelkapitän* of 10.(Pz)/SG 2, took off from his base at Niemes-South, in Bohemia, for his 704th, and final, operation. With him in the *'Gustav'* were his air-gunner (right) and his crew chief. When the mission was completed, Korol flew west to Kitzingen, in Germany, where all three surrendered to the Americans. The Stuka's war on the eastern front was finally over

APPENDICES

APPENDIX 1

COMMANDING OFFICERS

Stukageschwader 1

Hagen, *Oberst* Walter	22/6/41 to 1/43

I./StG 1

Kaubisch, *Hptm* Horst	17/6/43 to 18/10/43

II./StG 1

Keil, *Hptm* Anton	22/6/41 to 29/8/41 (†)
Zemsky, *Hptm* Johann	30/8/41 to 28/8/42 (†)
Schrepfer, *Hptm* Karl	? to 18/10/43

III./StG 1

Mahlke, *Hptm* Helmut	22/6/41 to 8/41
Gassmann, *Hptm* Peter	19/9/41 to 3/12/42
Nordmann, *Hptm* Theodor	10/12/42 to 27/3/43
Lang, *Hptm* Friedrich	4/43 to 18/10/43

Stukageschwader 2

Dinort, *Maj* Oskar	22/6/41 to 15/10/41
Hozzel, *Maj* Paul-Werner	16/10/41 to 13/2/43
Kupfer, *Maj* Dr Ernst	13/2/43 to 1/9/43
Stepp, *Obstlt* Hans-Karl	10/9/43 to 18/10/43

I./StG 2

Hitschhold, *Hptm* Hubertus	22/6/41 to 15/9/41
Neubert, *Hptm* Frank (acting)	15/9/41 to 1/42
Dilley, *Hptm* Bruno	1/42 to 7/43
Boerst, *Hptm* Alwin	7/43 to 18/10/43

II./StG 2

Schütte, *Hptm* Gerhard	6/1/42 to 2/42
Pekrun, *Hptm* Dieter	2/42 to 26/2/42
Kupfer, *Maj* Dr Ernst	27/2/42 to 12/2/43
Lehmann, *Hptm* Hans-Joachim (acting)	3/43 to 5/43
Stepp, *Maj* Hans-Karl	17/6/43 to 10/9/43
Otte, *Maj* Dr Maximilian	10/9/43 to 3/44

III./StG 2

Brücker, *Hptm* Heinrich	22/6/41 to 22/7/41
Steen, *Hptm* Ernst-Siegfried	7/8/41 to 23/9/41 (†)
Pressler, *Hptm* Gustav	24/9/41 to 31/3/43
Krauss, *Hptm* Walter	1/4/43 to 17/7/43 (†)
Rudel, *Hptm* Hans-Ulrich	19/7/43 to 18/10/43

Stukageschwader 3

I./StG 3

Schiller, *Hptm* Horst	2/43 to 2/6/43 (†)
Naumann, *Hptm* Helmut	19/6/43 to 7/43

III./StG 3

Jakob, *Hptm* Eberhard	6/43 to 18/10/43

Stukageschwader 5

IV.(St)LG 1

von Brauchitsch, *Hptm* Bernd	22/6/41 to 30/6/41
Blasig, *Hptm* Arnulf	1/7/41 to 27/1/42

I./StG 5

Blasig, *Hptm* Arnulf	27/1/42 to 22/6/42
Stepp, *Hptm* Hans-Karl	23/6/42 to 6/43
Kaubisch, *Hptm* Horst	6/43 to 17/6/43

I./StG 5 (new)

Mobüs, *Hptm* Martin	17/6/43 to 18/10/43

Stukageschwader 77

von Schönborn, *Oberst* Clemens *Graf*	22/6/41 to 20/7/42
Orthofer, *Maj* Alfons	25/7/42 to 12/10/42 (†)
Enneccerus, *Maj* Walter	13/10/42 to 20/2/43
Bruck, *Oberst* Helmut	20/2/43 to 18/10/43

I./StG 77

Bruck, *Hptm* Helmut	22/6/41 to 19/2/43
Henze, *Hptm* Karl	3/43 to 18/10/43

II./StG 77

Orthofer, *Maj* Alfons	22/6/41 to 26/6/42
Huhn, *Hptm* Kurt	1/7/42 to 1/4/43
Leicht, *Maj* Helmut	23/4/43 to 18/10/43

III./StG 77

Bode, *Hptm* Helmut	22/6/41 to 25/8/42
Jakob, *Hptm* Georg	26/8/42 to 1/12/42
Kieslich, *Hptm* Franz	1/12/42 to 18/10/43

APPENDIX 2

AWARD WINNERS

Date	Name	Unit	Position	Award	Fate
24/6/41	Lau, *Oblt* Lothar	8./StG 2	StaKa	KC	PoW
24/6/41	Neubert, *Oblt* Frank	2./StG 2	StaKa	KC	-
24/6/41	Pekrun, *Oblt* Dieter	StG 2	Adj	KC	-
24/6/41	Schwärzel, *Hptm* Günther	9./StG 2	StaKa	KC	DoW
14/7/41	Dinort, *Obstlt* Oskar	StG 2	GesK	OL	-
16/7/41	Mahlke, *Hptm* Helmut	III./StG 1	GpK	KC	-
30/8/41	Schairer, *Oblt* Hartmut	7./StG 1	StKa	KC	KiA
4/9/41	Bock, *Stabsfw* Albert	StG 2	-	KC	PoW
4/9/41	Blasig, *Hptm* Arnulf	IV.(St)/LG 1	GpK	KC	-
4/9/41	Bruck, *Hptm* Helmut	I./StG 77	GpK	KC	-
17/9/41	Nordmann, *Lt* Theodor	III./StG 1	-	KC	KiA
5/10/41	Boerst, *Oblt* Alwin	I./StG 2	-	KC	KiA
5/10/41	Freitag, *Oblt* Bruno	3./StG 2	StaKa	KC	-
10/10/41	Bode, *Hptm* Helmuth	III./StG 77	GpK	KC	-
10/10/41	Pfeiffer, *Oblt* Johannes	12.(St)/LG 1	StaKa	KC	-
17/10/41	Steen, *Hptm* Ernst-Siegfried	III./StG 2	GpK	KC*	KiA
23/11/41	Kupfer, *Hptm* Dr Ernst	2./StG 2	StaKa	KC	KAS
23/11/41	Lang, *Oblt* Friedrich	1./StG 2	StaKa	KC	-
23/11/41	Lehmann, *Oblt* Hans-Joachim	8./StG 2	StaKa	KC	-
23/11/41	Orthofer, *Hptm* Alfons	II./StG 77	GpK	KC	DoW
23/11/41	Ruppert, *Oblt* Hermann	6./StG 77	StaKa	KC	KiA
31/12/41	Hitschhold, *Maj* Hubertus	I./StG 2	GpK	OL	-
6/1/42	Hachtel, *Ofw* August	II./StG 1	-	KC	-
6/1/42	von Malapert-Neufville, *Oblt* Robert-Georg *Freiherr*	5./StG 1	StaKa	KC	KiA
6/1/42	Rudel, *Oblt* Hans-Ulrich	III./StG 2	TO	KC	-
24/1/42	Waldhauser, *Oblt* Johann	9./StG 77	StaKa	KC	KiA
4/2/42	Kaiser, *Oblt* Wilhelm	III./StG 2	Adj	KC	-
4/2/42	Pressler, *Hptm* Gustav	III./StG 2	GpK	KC	-
4/2/42	Stepp, *Oblt* Hans-Karl	7./StG 2	StaKa	KC	-
4/2/42	Zemsky, *Hptm* Johann	II./StG 1	GpK	KC	KiA
16/2/42	Sattler, *Oblt* Hans-Karl	8./StG 77	StaKa	KC	-
17/2/42	Hagen, *Obstlt* Walter	StG 1	Ges.K	OL	-
19/3/42	Rieger, *Oblt* Joachim	5./StG 1	StaKa	KC*	KiA
5/4/42	Otte, *Oblt* Dr Maximilian	9./StG 2	StaKa	KC	KiA
5/4/42	Platzer, *Oblt* Friedrich	3/StG 2	StaKa	KC*	KiA
5/4/42	Schmalz, *Lt* Alfons	II./StG 2	-	KC	DoW
27/4/42	Jakob, *Oblt* Georg	2./StG 77	StaKa	KC	-
27/4/42	Weigel, *Stabsfw* Rudolf	III./StG 77	-	KC	MiA
15/5/42	Jaekel, *Lt* Egbert	I./StG 2	-	KC	KiA
25/5/42	Bauhaus, *Hptm* Gerhard	8./StG 77	StaKa	KC	DoW
25/5/42	Gassmann, *Hptm* Peter	III./StG 1	GpK	KC	-
4/6/42	Lion, *Oblt* Karl-Hermann	9./StG 1	StaKa	KC	-
7/6/42	Stimpl, *Oblt* Walter	6./StG 77	StaKa	KC	-
8/6/42	von Malapert-Neufville, *Hptm* Robert-Georg *Freiherr*	5./StG 1	StaKa	OL*	KiA

Date	Name	Unit	Position	Award	Fate
19/6/42	Graber, *Lt* Heinz	7./StG 2	StaKa	KC	KiA
19/6/42	Schrepfer, *Oblt* Karl	6./StG 1	StaKa	KC	KiA
15/7/42	Amelung, *Hptm* Heinz-Günter	StG 77	Ia	KC	-
15/7/42	Henze, *Oblt* Karl	1./StG 77	StaKa	KC	-
13/8/42	Hanne, *Lt* Erich	7./StG 1	StaKa	KC	KiA
3/9/42	Jochens, *Ofw* Hermann	StG 2	-	KC	PoW
3/9/42	Leicht, *Hptm* Helmut	2./StG 77	StKa	KC	MiA
3/9/42	Schmidt, *Hptm* Otto	7./StG 77	StaKa	KC	-
3/9/42	Zemsky, *Hptm* Johann	II./StG 1	GpK	OL*	KiA
19/9/42	Bevernis, *Ofw* Heinz	7./StG 1	Wop/AG	KC*	KiA
19/9/42	Fick, *Hptm* Ernst	6./StG 2	StaKa	KC*	KiA
15/10/42	Diekwisch, *Lt* Erwin-Peter	III./StG 1	Adj	KC	-
3/11/42	Bleckl, *Oblt* Karl	7./StG 1	StaKa	KC	-
3/11/42	Reusch, *Oblt* Ernst-Christian	5./StG 1	StaKa	KC	DoW
16/11/42	Janke, *Hptm* Karl	7./StG 2	StaKa	KC	-
16/11/42	Kaubisch, *Hptm* Horst	9./StG 77	StaKa	KC	KiA
16/11/42	Wutka, *Oblt* Bernhard	8./StG 2	StaKa	KC	KiA
21/11/42	Lang, *Hptm* Friedrich	1./StG 2	StaKa	OL	-
25/11/42	Fischer, *Hptm* Heinz	9./StG 1	StaKa	KC*	KiA
27/11/42	Fitzner, *Lt* Karl	5./StG 77	StaKa	KC	KiA
27/11/42	Jauernik, *Stabsfw* Georg	II./StG 77	-	KC	KAS
28/11/42	Boerst, *Hptm* Alwin	3./StG 2	StaKa	OL	KiA
23/12/42	Schmid, *Lt* Günther	5./StG 2	StaKa	KC	KiA
23/12/42	Stahl, *Lt* Hendrik	III./StG 2	-	KC	-
30/12/42	Czekay, *Oblt* Richard	I./StG 2	Adj	KC	-
5/1/43	Kieslich, *Oblt* Franz	7./StG 77	StaKa	KC	-
8/1/43	Dilley, *Hptm* Bruno	I./StG 2	GpK	OL	-
8/1/43	Kupfer, *Major* Dr Ernst	II./StG 2	GpK	OL	KAS
22/1/43	Langhart, *Oblt* Theordor	8./StG 77	StaKa	KC*	KiA
22/1/43	Stifter, *Lt* Kurt	III./StG 77	Adj	KC*	KiA
26/1/43	Pressler, *Hptm* Gustav	III./StG 2	GpK	OL	-
19/2/43	Bruck, *Hptm* helmut	I./StG 77	GpK	OL	-
19/2/43	Gläser, *Oblt* Alexander	4./StG 77	StaKa	KC	-
19/2/43	Langkopf, *Ofw* Paul	I./StG 77	-	KC	-
19/2/43	Weihrauch, *Ofw* Werner	I./StG 77	-	KC	-
4/3/43	Herling, *Oblt* Wilfried	7./StG 2	StaKa	KC	KiA
17/3/43	Huhn, *Hptm* Kurt	II./StG 77	GpK	KC	-
17/3/43	Nordmann, *Oblt* Theodor	III./StG 1	GpK	OL	KiA
24/3/43	Langbehn, *Hptm* Joachim	5./StG 2	StaKa	KC*	KiA
3/4/43	Huber, *Ofw* Siegfried	III./StG 2	-	KC*	KiA
3/4/43	Rick, *Oblt* Kurt	2./StG 77	StaKa	KC*	KiA
3/4/43	Schalanda, *Hptm* Hans	III./StG 1	-	KC	KiA
14/4/43	Hozzel, *Obstlt* Paul-Werner	StG 2	GesK	OL	-
14/4/43	Rudel, *Hptm* Hans-Ulrich	1./StG 2	StaKa	OL	-
16/4/43	Bromen, *Ltn* Wilhelm	II./StG 2	-	KC	-
16/4/43	Fritzsche, *Oblt* Immo	8./StG 2	StaKa	KC	DoW
16/4/43	Klüber, *Oblt* Wilhelm	8./StG 1	StaKa	KC	KiA
16/4/43	Kuffner, *Oblt* Andreas	II./StG 2	-	KC	KiA
10/5/43	Hörner, *Lt* Willi	7./StG 2	StaKa	KC	KiA
22/5/43	Schubert, *Ofw* Gustav	III./StG 1	-	KC	KiA

Date	Name	Unit	Position	Award	Fate
25/5/43	Roell, *Hptm* Werner	StG 77	-	KC	-
20/6/43	Pape, *Hptm* Kurt-Albert	3./StG 5	StaKa	KC	KiA
22/7/43	Peter, *Uffz* Erich	StG 2	-	KC	KiA
31/7/43	Lorenz, *Hptm* Friedrich	1./StG 1	StaKa	KC*	KiA
19/8/43	Stein, *Ofw* Werner	I./StG 2	Wop/AG	KC	-
19/9/43	Krumminga, *Lt* Hans	III./StG 2	TO	KC	KiA
19/9/43	Plenzat, *Ofw* Kurt	I./StG 2	-	KC	-
9/10/43	Jungclaussen, *Oblt* Heinz	1./StG 2	StaKa	KC	KiA
9/10/43	Roka, *Oblt* Franz	6./StG 1	StaKa	KC	MiA
29/2/44	Jenster, *Ofw* Jakob	II./StG 2(Pz)	-	KC	-

Key

GesK	– *Geschwaderkommodore*
GpK	– *Gruppenkommandeur*
StaKa	– *Staffelkapitän* (or *Staffelführer*)
Adj	– Adjutant
Ia	– Operations Officer
TO	– Technical (Engineering) Officer
Wop/AG	– Wireless operator/Air gunner
KiA	– Killed in Action
MiA	– Missing in Action
KAS	– Killed on Active Service
DAS	– Died on Active Service
DoW	– Died of Wounds
PoW	– Prisoner of War
OL	– Oak Leaves
KC	– Knight's Cross
*	– awarded posthumously

Notes

– Several of the above awards were conferred shortly *after* the recipient had been taken off operations with the unit listed and appointed to a staff or training post.

– A dash behind a *Geschwader* designation in the Position column indicates that the recipient flew as a member of the *Geschwader's Stab* or reconnaissance *Staffel*.

– A dash behind a *Gruppe* designation in the Position column indicates that the recipient flew in one of the *Gruppe's* three component *Staffeln*, but not in a position of command.

– A dash in the Fate column indicates that the recipient survived the war.

COLOUR PLATES

1
Ju 87D-3 'A5+DB' of Stab I./StG1, Kursk, July 1943
One of Hauptmann Horst Kaubisch's *Gruppenstab* machines is depicted here shortly after the unit's redesignation from I./StG 5 to become the 'new' I./StG 1 (see text) as part of the aerial build-up for Operation *Zitadelle*, the forthcoming Battle of Kursk. Note StG 1's code combination 'A5' freshly applied in one-fifth scale on the overpainted patch ahead of the fuselage cross.

2
Ju 87R-1 '6G+HS' of 5./StG 1, Minsk area, July 1941
Although having operated as II./StG 1 for a full year, the machines of this unit still bore the fuselage codes of III./StG 51 – their original *Gruppe* identity prior to redesignation back in July 1940 (see e.g. *Osprey Combat Aircraft 1 – Junkers Ju 87 Stukageschwader 1937-1941*, Profiles 11 and 20). Note also that unlike the Luftwaffe's fighters in the east, which eschewed red individual markings in order to avoid confusion with the red Soviet star, Stukas still carried red *Staffel* trim (at least during the early stages of *Barbarossa*).

3
Ju 87D-3 'J9+LK' of 7./StG 1, Volkhov front, January 1943
StG 1's third *Gruppe* also retained the codes of its previous identity. This unit had originally been activated as I.(St)/186(T) for service aboard the aircraft carrier *Graf Zeppelin* (hence the now decidedly incongruous anchor incorporated in the *Staffel* badge!), before being redesignated III./StG 1 in July 1940 (see *Osprey Combat Aircraft 1*, profiles 12 and 28). During the early weeks of 1943, III./StG 1 came under the control of both *Luftwaffenkommando Ost* on the central sector and *Luftflotte* 1 on the northern sector. Note the temporary white winter finish worn for operations over the Lake Ilmen area.

4
Ju 87D-3 'J9+MK' of 7./StG 1, Bryansk, August 1943
Some 7. *Staffel* aircraft, including the somewhat worn 'MK' depicted here, were still wearing the unit's 'Helmet and Anchor' badge when operating against partisans in the forests around Bryansk in the aftermath of *Zitadelle*. References suggest that the emblem finally disappeared at the time of the Stuka units' wholesale incorporation into the *Schlacht* arm in October 1943.

5
Ju 87D-1 'T6+AA' of the Geschwaderstab StG 2 'Immelmann', Southern sector, circa July 1942
The black and white 'Crusader's cross of Jesau' *Geschwaderstab* shield, together with the last two of the fuselage code ('AA') and the numeral '1' on the wheel-spat, all point to this being the mount of *Geschwaderkommodore* Major Paul-Werner Hozzel, as flown during StG 2's operations in support of 6. *Armee's* advance on Stalingrad during the summer of 1942. Note the *Geschwaderstab* designation 'A' and the spinner tip both in blue.

6
Ju 87D-1 'T6+CB' of Stab I./StG 2 'Immelmann', Oblivskaya, July 1942
Also depicted during the advance across the Ukraine in the high summer of 1942, this is the machine of I./StG 2's *Gruppenkommandeur* Hauptmann Bruno Dilley. Whereas the *Gruppe* designator 'B' is in white (as is the numeral '1' on the wheel-spat), both the individual letter 'C' and the background to StG 2's famous 'Scottie dog' badge are in the green of a *Gruppenstab* aircraft. An extra refinement is the command chevron added to the white surround of the disc.

7
Ju 87B-2 'T6+NH' of 1./StG 2 'Immelmann', Lyck/East Prussia, June 1941
One of the machines employed by StG 2 in its first major eastern front operation – the twin 'cauldron' battles of Bialystok and Minsk – only days into *Barbarossa*, and while still based on German soil. 'NH' had seen action in the Balkans campaign, as witness the unusual green finish of the cowling and rudder (a result of the botched removal of the Balkans yellow theatre markings – see *Osprey Combat Aircraft 6 – Junkers Ju 87 Stukageschwader of North Africa and the Mediterranean* Profiles 6, 27 and 28 for their overpainting in a non-standard hue).

8
Ju 87D-2 'T6+CH' of 1./StG 2 'Immelmann', Achtirskaya, June 1942
A year almost exactly to the day after the launch of *Barbarossa*, StG 2 returned to the eastern front from a brief period of rest and re-equipment in Austria ready for the summer offensive of 1942. It first staged to Achtirskaya, east of Kursk, before transferring forward to support the ground troops' advance on Voronezh. To facilitate the frequent moves from one base to the next, the *Geschwader* had been assigned its own group of some 40 transport gliders, and a third of the *Geschwader's* Ju 87s were deployed as tugs. 'CH' is one such, as shown by the tow-hook attachment behind the tail wheel.

9
Ju 87D-3 'T6+HH' of 1./StG 2 'Immelmann', Gorlovka, February 1943
Another '*Dora*' of 1./StG 2, this particular aircraft – minus towing hook – is reported to be the machine

flown by the unit's *Staffelkapitän*, Oberleutnant Hans-Ulrich Rudel, when he completed his 1000th operation on 10 February 1943 during the fighting along the Donetz front south of Kharkov. This may, in fact, have been a replacement machine, as Rudel is also known to have flown 'AH' during the winter of 1942/43.

10
Ju 87D-3 'T6+AK' of 2./StG 2 'Immelmann', Morosovskaya, November 1942

One of Rudel's fellow *Staffelkapitäne* as the Battle of Stalingrad approached its climax was 2./StG 2's Oberleutnant Armin Thiede, whose well-known winter-camouflaged *'Dora'* is shown here. Note the abundant use of the red 2. *Staffel* trim for the background to I. *Gruppe's* 'Scottie dog' badge, as well as for the spinner tip and the dive-bomber's individual letter on the aft fuselage and (just visible) the front of the mainwheel spat.

11
Ju 87D-1 'T6+AC' of *Stab* II./StG 2 'Immelmann', Gostkino, circa April 1942

When a replacement II./StG 2 was formed at the beginning of 1942 (see text) Hauptmann Dr Ernst Kupfer, the first *Kommandeur* to lead the unit into action, introduced a new *Gruppe* badge. Depicting the 'Horseman of Bamberg', it was based on the coat-of-arms of Dr Kupfer's home town. Following the example of I./StG 2's 'Scottie dog', it was applied to aircraft of the *Gruppenstab* and all three component *Staffeln* in the respective background colours of green, white, red and yellow. On the *Kommandeur's* own mount the emblem was further enhanced by a command chevron.

12
Ju 87D-3 'T6+BM' of 4./StG 2 'Immelmann', Southern sector, autumn 1943

The overpainting of the *Staffel* badge on this *'Dora'* would suggest that it was operating in the post-*Zitadelle* period when many distinctive unit emblems were being removed for reasons of security. This still leaves a wealth of other markings, including the white spinner tip, individual name *Brunhilde* on the engine cowling, number '2' on the wheel-spat and a diagonal stripe on the rudder. This latter – used either as an aid for recognition or to indicate a command aircraft – was a not uncommon feature on eastern front Stukas. Note, too, that whereas many machines had their wheel-spats (or parts thereof) removed during the winter months, 'BM' is, for some reason, minus its mainwheel leg fairings.

13
Ju 87D-3 'T6+AN' of 5./StG 2 'Immelmann', Kerch IV, Crimea, April 1943

With its 'Horseman of Bamberg' badge well in evidence, 'AN' is almost certainly the machine flown by the *Staffelkapitän* of 5./StG 2, Oberleutnant Günther Schmid. Note the numeral '1' on the mainwheel spat and the yellow segment to the rear of it, which was a device to help *Staffel* members re-formate on their leader after the dive. Note, too, that this is not the same *Bärli* as the machine shown in the photograph on page 45, when (presumably) the same pilot was flying as No 2 in Hauptmann Dr Kupfer's *Gruppenstab*.

14
Ju 87B-2 'T6+AD' of *Stab* III./StG 2 'Immelmann', Tyrkovo, September 1941

Bearing the 'Hlinka Cross' *Gruppe* shield, 'AD' was the regular mount of III./StG 2's *Kommandeur*, Hauptmann Siegfried Steen. He flew it on his 300th operational mission – an attack on the Soviet Baltic Fleet in Kronstadt harbour, on 23 September 1941. But on landing back at Tyrkovo he stood 'AD' on its nose and so had to 'borrow' the machine – and air-gunner – of his then *Gruppen*-TO, a certain Hans-Ulrich Rudel, to fly a second sortie against the same target, from which he failed to return.

15
Ju 87D-3 'S7+FH' of 1./StG 3, Crimea, summer 1943

I./StG 3 only saw service on the eastern front from February to July 1943 (although it would return to Russia the following year after redesignation as a *Schlachtgruppe*). 'FH' was one of the 46 *'Doras'* equipping the unit when it arrived in the Crimea fresh from refurbishment in Germany. More than a quarter of that number would be lost before the *Gruppe* returned to the Mediterranean theatre.

16
Ju 87D-5 'S7+CS' of 8./StG 3, Crimea, October 1943

When III./StG 3 arrived on the eastern front in June 1943, the move from the Mediterranean was permanent. After briefly serving under its own parent *Geschwaderstab* on the central sector, the *Gruppe* took I./StG 3's place in the Crimea from September onwards. 'CS' was among the unit's first D-5s – note the long-barrelled 20 mm Mauser MG 151s in the leading edges of the extended-span wings.

17
Ju 87R-2 'L1+FV' of 11.(St)/LG 1, Kirkenes, Norway, June 1941

Representative of the only Stuka presence north of the Arctic Circle at the start of *Barbarossa*, 'FV' carries 11. *Staffel's* 'pitchfork-wielding devil astride a bomb' badge on its engine cowling, but the eastern front theatre markings appear to be confined to just yellow underwing tips.

18
Ju 87D-3 'L1-BB' of *Stab* I./StG 5, Alakurtti, Finland, circa February 1943

When IV.(St)/LG 1 was redesignated to become I./StG 5 early in 1942, the unit retained its original 'L1' *Geschwader* designator (albeit subsequently reduced to one-fifth size as seen here), but replaced the now anachronistic IV. *Gruppe Stab* and *Staffel* code letters (E, U, V and W) with their standard I. *Gruppe* equivalents (B, H, K and L). 'BB' is typical of the aircraft flown by I./StG 5 during its many strikes against the Murmansk railway in the winter of 1942/43.

19
Ju 87D-3 'S2+AA' of the *Geschwaderstab* StG 77, Poltava, autumn 1943

Pictured in post-*Zitadelle* livery, this is reportedly the aircraft flown by Kommodore Oberst Helmut Bruck just prior to the *Geschwader's* transition from StG 77 to SG 77. Note the numeral '1' on the wheel-spat and the diagonal white stripe on the rudder denoting a command machine. The unit's distinctive badge, however (a partitioned shield design used by every *Gruppe* and *Staffel* within the *Geschwader*, each with its own motif superimposed), is no longer in evidence.

20
Ju 87D-3 'S7+ML' of 3./StG 77, Kuban, summer 1942

The upper segments of the shields carried by all I./StG 77 machines were white – the *Gruppe* colour. And in the case of 3. *Staffel* aircraft, the individual device depicted on the yellow field below was an owl's head, as partly visible here. During their brief spell of operations over the Kuban and northern Caucasus, most of the unit's '*Doras*' had their wheel spats removed to facilitate taxiing on the arid, dusty landing grounds.

21
Ju 87D-3 'S2+BC' of *Stab* II./StG 77, Taganrog, September 1942

Although the red upper segment of the shield as sported by all II. *Gruppe* aircraft is clearly visible, the *Stab's* chosen motif – an heraldic lion rampant in black on the yellow background – is all but obscured by heavy exhaust staining. Otherwise, 'BC' carries a textbook set of markings, including a small white individual letter 'B' repeated on the front of the wheel-spats.

22
Ju 87B-2 'S2+KM' of 4./StG 77, Smolensk area, July 1941

'KM', one of the 39 '*Bertas*' fielded by II./StG 77 at the start of *Barbarossa*, also displays II. *Gruppe's* red and yellow partitioned shield, this time with the cockerel of 4. *Staffel* superimposed. After operating on the central sector during the opening weeks of the hostilities against the Soviet Union, StG 77 would spend the remainder of the war flying almost entirely on the southern sector.

23
Ju 87D-3 'S2+NP' of 6./StG 77, Southern sector, October 1943

The absence of both a *Staffel* badge and any undercarriage fairings would seem to indicate that this decidedly grubby '*Dora*' of 6./StG 77 was having to cope with the autumn mud of the Ukraine in 1943. II./StG 77 was redesignated to become III./SG 10 on 18 October, and it would convert to Fw 190s early in 1944.

24
Ju 87B-2 'F1+EM' of 7./StG 77, Woskrzenice, Poland, June 1941

Another *Gruppe* that clung to the codes of its former identity was III./StG 77, which had been created by redesignating the Do 17-equipped II./KG 76 in July 1940. Not only did this unit retain the 'F1' *Geschwader* designator of KG 76, it also continued to use the Standard C, M, N and P codes of II. *Gruppe*. Thus, at the beginning of Operation *Barbarossa*, there were two *Gruppen* within StG 77 based on the same airfield in Poland and using the same last letters in their fuselage codes – see e.g. 7. *Staffel's* 'EM' depicted here, and 4. *Staffel's* 'KM' (Profile 22). This duplication reportedly lasted until the units' re-equipment with '*Doras*' in 1942.

25
Ju 87D-3 'White 9' of *Grupul* 3, Rumanian Air Force, Bagerovo (Kerch VI), Crimea, August 1943

One of the first batch of 45 '*Doras*' handed over to the Rumanians by the Luftwaffe – note the aircraft's overpainted tail swastika – to enable them to set up *Grupul* 3 (comprising three *Escadrilas*, Nos 73, 81 and 85, of 15 aircraft each), this particular machine – nicknamed *Hai Pusa* ('Go, Pusa') – had a very short operational career with the Rumanian Air Force. Arriving in the Crimea sometime in mid-August 1943, it was lost to Soviet anti-aircraft fire on 2 September.

26
Ju 87D-5 'White 861' of *Grupul* 6, Rumanian Air Force, Husi, July 1944

Although bearing a superficially similar individual name to the machine above, aircraft 861 *Hai noroc!* is a cannon-armed D-5 that reportedly belonged to *Grupul* 6. Note the even more crudely overpainted Luftwaffe markings, the smaller fuselage cross and the Rumanian tricolour on the upper portion of the rudder. *Grupul* 6's three component *Escadrilas* were numbered 74, 86 and 87. The equally crudely applied three-digit rudder numeral may therefore possibly identify this as aircraft No 1 of 86 Sqn – and could that black cat perhaps be the short-lived squadron badge?

27
Ju 87B-2 B.601, Hungarian Air Force, Winter 1941/42

The first two Stukas (B.601 and B.602) delivered to the Hungarians were renovated ex-Luftwaffe Ju 87B-2s. B.601 is seen here in its initial finish and markings, the latter consisting of tricolour chevrons in Hungary's national colours of red, white and green carried on the vertical tail surfaces and above and below each wing. The ten '*Bertas*' (and four elderly '*Antons*') supplied to Hungary in 1941/42 were employed almost exclusively in training roles.

28
Ju 87D-3 B.634 of 102/2 Dive-bomber Squadron, Hungarian Air Force, Southern sector, autumn 1943

Bearing definitive Hungarian wartime markings (a combination of a white cross on a black square on fuselage and wings, plus a tricolour segment on the rudder), the '*Doras*' of 102/2 Squadron flew for some three months under the tactical command of II./StG 77. Although not seen here, the unit even adopted a badge similar to those carried by machines of StG 77. Its motif – a monkey holding, or hurling a coconut – inevitably led to 102/2's nickname as the 'Baboon' or 'Coconut' squadron.

29
Ju 87R-2 'White 8' of the Bulgarian Air Force, circa autumn 1943

One of the R-2s supplied to Bulgaria from ex-Luftwaffe stock during August-September 1943 for use as operational trainers.

30
Ju 87D-5 'White 24' of 1/2 'Storm' Regiment, Bulgarian Air Force, summer 1944

Some of Bulgaria's 24+ operational D-5s saw brief service in action against anti-Fascist partisans both in their own homeland and neighbouring Yugoslavia during the summer of 1944.

31
Ju 87D-5 OK-XAB of the Slovakian Air Force, circa spring 1944

This is believed to be the second machine (note small numeral '2' at base of rudder) of the first batch of three *'Doras'* supplied to Slovakia in the spring of 1944. The prominent fuselage lettering may well have been the delivery markings applied in Germany prior to despatch (OK-XAA to OK-XAC, with OK being the pre-war international civil code for Czechoslovakia). One source suggests that Slovakia's 'operational' Ju 87s were later repainted with fuselage codes commencing 'B-1'.

32
Ju 87R-2 'White 2' of 1.kr.S.St., Eichwalde/East Prussia, circa September 1944

Like Bulgaria (see Profile 29), Croatia also received a small batch of long-retired, ex-Luftwaffe Ju 87R-2s. Unlike the Bulgarians, however, the Croats are on record as having used their machines against the Red Army. This final profile is a reconstruction of earlier published artworks, and purports to show the markings carried by Croatia's Stukas during their operations over the East Prussian/ Polish border regions in the early autumn of 1944.

INDEX

References to illustrations are shown in **bold**. Plates are shown with page and caption locators in brackets.

Andorfer, Lt Anton 79
Arctic operations 19, 37-39, 70

Bauer, Lt Herbert 42
Bauhaus, Hptm Gerhard 46-47
Bevernis, Ofw Heinz 49
Black Sea operations 21-22, 23, 31, 36-37, 48, 75-76
Blasig, Hptm Arnulf 19, 20, 38
Bode, Hptm Helmut 14, 23
Brest-Litovsk fortress citadel 9-10
bridges as targets **10**, **15**, 15
Bruck, Obst Helmut 21, **23**, 23, **33**, 94
Bryansk pocket 25
Bulgarian Air Force **29**, **30**(63, 95), 83-84, **84**

Caucasus Mountains 47, **48**, 48
Cholm pocket 40, 41, 43
convoys PQ 12 and 13: 38
Crimea operations 22-23, 31-33, 79-80 *see also* Sevastopol
Croatian Ju 87 operations (*1.kr.S.St*) 85

Demyansk pocket 39-40, 41, 43, 49
Diekwisch, Oblt Erwin-Peter 69
Dietrich, Dr Otto 25
Dilley, Hptm Bruno **40**, 40, 92
Dinort, Obstlt 'Onkel' Oskar 12, 14, 17
Dugino 39

Fick, Hptm Ernst 51
Fischer, Hptm Heinz 50-51
Fitzner, Hptm Karl 72
Focke-Wulf Fw 190: 76-77

German Army: *Armee*, 6. 21, 51, 53, 54, 64; *Armee*, 9. 74; *Armee*, 11. 12, 22, 31, 34;*Armee*, 17. 46; *Armeekorps*, XXIII 26; *Armeekorps*, XXXVI. 19; Army Group 'A' 45, 47, 48, 51, 65, 66; Army Group 'B' 45, 47; Army Group Centre 23, 39, 83; Army Group South 14, 31; *Korps*, XXXXVII armoured 11; *Korps*, LVII armoured 11; Mountain Corps, XIX. 19, 20; Mountain Divisions, 1. and 4. 47; *Panzerarmee*, 1. 23, 46, 75; *Panzerarmee*, 2. 27-28; *Panzerarmee*, 4. 28, 51; *Panzerarmee*, 8. 75; *Panzerdivision*, 1. 25; *Panzerdivision*, 16. 52; *Panzerdivision*, 17. 13-14; *Panzergruppe* 2: 7, 9, 11, 12, 25; *Panzergruppe* 3: 7, 9, 11, 25; *Panzergruppe* 4: 25; *Panzerpionierbataillon* 62: 28; *SS-Panzerdivision 'Das Reich'*, 2. 39; SS-*Panzergrenadier* division, 3. 15; Waffen-SS **64**, 67
Göring, *Reichsmarshall* Hermann 31, 46

Hagen, Obst Walter 14, 23-24, **49**
Hanne, Lt Erich 50
Haugk, Ofw Werner 36
Hentschel, Ofw Erwin **66**, **74**, 75
Hitler, Adolf: and Axis air forces 78, 79, 82, 84; in 1942 12, 20, 25, 27, 28, 39, 44, 45-46; in 1943 67, 68, 69, 70, 71, 72, **74**
Hozzel, Maj Paul-Werner 39, 67, 68, 92
Hrabak, Obstlt Dietrich **74**
Hungarian Air Force **27**, **28**(62, 94-95), **81**, 81-83, **82**

Italian Expeditionary Corps in Russia (CSIR), 371o *Squadriglia* 22

Jaekel, Oblt Egbert 72-73
Jenster, Ofw Jakob 86-87
Jentzsch, Ofw Fritz 'Tubby' 73
Joswig, Ofw Wilhelm 14
Jungclaussen, Lt Heinz **4**, **54**, 55
Junkers Ju 52/3m 29
Junkers Ju 87 Stuka **4**, 6, **26**, **38**, **40**, **43**, **50**, **52**; StG 77: **13**, **14**, **22**, **29**, **35**, **48**, **76**
Junkers Ju 87B **7**, **10**, **12**, **21**, **25**, **29**, **47**, **81**; Ju 87B-1 **24**; Ju 87B-2 **14**, **28**, **7**(57, 92), **14**(59, 93), **22**, **24**(61, 94), **27**(62, 94)
Junkers Ju 87D 29, **38**, 40, **41**, **48**, **49**, **55**, **77**, **82**; OK-XAC **85**; Rumanian **78**, **79**, 79, **80**; 'S2+HK' **53**; 'S2+NM' **32**; StG 77:

INDEX

32, **46**, **53**, **68**; 'T6+KM' **41**; 'White 46' **84**
Ju 87D-1 **5, 6**(57, 92), **11**(58, 93), **73**
Ju 87D-2 **8**(57, 92)
Ju 87D-3 **64**; 'A5+DB' **1**(56, 92); B.634 **28**(62, 95); 'J9+BM' **50**; 'J9+LK' **3**(56, 92); 'J9+LL' **27**; 'J9+MK' **4**(56, 92); 'L1+BB' **18**(60, 93-94); 'S2+AA' **19**(60, 94); 'S2+BC' **21**(61, 94); 'S2+NP' **23**(61, 94); 'S7+FH' **15**(59, 93); 'S7+ML' **20**(60, 94); 'T6+AK' **10**(58, 93); 'T6+AN' **13**(59, 93); 'T6+BC' **45**; 'T6+BM' **12**(58, 93); 'T6+DC' **52**; 'T6+HH' **9**(58, 92-93); 'White 9' **25**(62, 94)
Ju 87D-5 **16**(59, 93), **26**(62, 94), **30, 31**(63, 95), **71**, **73**, **77**
Junkers Ju 87G **65**, 65, 66-67, **86**, **87**
Junkers Ju 87R 19, **20**; Ju 87R-1 **8**, **2**(56, 92); Ju 87R-2 **19**, **17**(60, 93), **29**, **32**(63, 95), **70**

Kalinin 25-26
Karpovka 54-55
Kather, Ofw 40
Keil, Hptm Anton 24
Kerch 31, 32-33, 68, 79
Kharkov 33-34, 67-68, 71, 75
Korol, Lt Anton **87**
Krauss, Maj Walter 73
Kresken, Oblt 39
Kronstadt **15**, 15, **16**, 16-18, **17**, **18**, **42**, 42
Kuban peninsula 65, 66-67, 79-80
Kupfer, Maj Dr Ernst **30**, 30, 41, **51**, 93
Kursk 70-72, **71**

Lang, Maj Friedrich 71
Langbehn, Hptm Joachim 55
Leicht, Oblt Helmut 11
Leningrad 15, 41-42
Lorenz, Hptm Friedrich 72
Luftwaffe *Stukageschwader*
(St)/LG 1: IV.(St)/LG 1 (later I./StG 5) 18-21, **19**, **20**, 37; 11.(St)/LG 1: **20**, **17**(60, 93)
SG 1 (formerly StG 1) 77
SG 2 (formerly StG 2) 77; III./SG 2: 86; 10.(Pz)/SG 2: 87
SG 3 and SG 5 (formerly StG 3 and StG 5) 77
SG 77 (formerly StG 77) 77; 10.(Pz)/SG 77: 87
StG 1 (later SG 1) 9, 12, 14, 23-24, 26, 27-28, 71, 74, 77; I./StG 1 70; I./StG 1, *Stab* **1**(56, 92); II./StG 1: **7**, 8, 23, **25**, 29, 31, 42-43, **50**, 51, 52, 55, 67, 68, **69**, 69, 74; III./StG 1: 7, 8-9, 10-11, 13, 23, 28-29, 40, 41-42, 49-50, 51, 71, **72**, 72; 5./StG 1: **2**(56, 92); 7./StG 1: **49**, **50**, **3**, **4**(56, 92); 8./StG 1: **43**; 9./StG 1: 10-11, **27**, **40**, 69; (Pz.J.St.)/StG 1: 69; *Stab* 7, **49**
StG 2 (later SG 2) 'Immelmann' 9, 10, 12, 14, 15, **16**, 16-17, 23-25, 26, 27, 29, 42, 43-44, **44**, 45, 51, 52, 55, 68, 71, 72, 74-75, **77**, 77; I./StG 2: 7, 11, **15**, 15, 25-26, 28-29, 40-41, 42, 44, 51, 52, 54, 55, 67, 68-69, 73; I./StG 2, *Stab* **52**, **6**(57, 92); I.(*Eins.*)./StG 2: 55; II./StG 2 (later III./StG 3) **30**, 30, 41-42, 52, 55, 67, 68-69; II./StG 2, *Stab* **52**, **11**(58, 93), **73**; II./StG 2(Pz) 86-87; III./StG 2: 7, 11, 15, 16, 29, 31, 39, 42, **66**, **71**, **73**, 73-74; III./StG 2, *Stab* 16, 17-18, **14**(59, 93); 1./StG 2: 53, **7-9**(57-58, 92-93); 2./StG 2: **48**, **10**(58,
93); 4./StG 2: **41**, **12**(58, 93); 5./StG 2: **13**(59, 93); *Ergänzungsstaffel* 30, 48; *Kommando* Jungclaussen **4**, **54**, 55; (*Pz.J.St.*)/StG 2: 69; *Stab* 7, 39, 44, **45**, 55, **5**(57, 92); *Stukaverband Kupfer* 68
StG 3 (later SG 3) 77; I./StG 3: 68; III./StG 3: 30, 70; 1./StG 3: **15**(59, 93); 8./StG 3: **16**(59, 93)
StG 5 (later SG 5) 77; I./StG 5 (formerly IV.(St)/LG 1, later I./StG 1) 37-38, **38**, 69-70, 70; I./StG 5, *Stab* **18**(60, 93-94), **70**; 4./StG 5: 70
StG 77 (later SG 77) **10**, 10, 12, **13**, 14, 21-23, 25, 26, 32-33, 34, 35, 36, 45, 46-47, 71, 75, 76, 77; I./StG 77: 7, 9, 14, **26**, 29, 31, **32**, 32, 47, 52, **53**, 67, **68**, 68, 75, **76**, 83; I./StG 77, *Stab* **29**; II./StG 77: 7, 9, 14, 29, **32**, 32, 47, **67**, 68, 75, 82; II./StG 77, *Stab* **22**, **21**(61, 94); III./StG 77: 7, 9, 14, 29, 31, 32, 33, 34, 52, 75; 1./StG 77: **32**; 2./StG 77: **53**; 3./StG 77: **46**, **20**(60, 94); 4./StG 77: **21**, **22**, **28**, **32**, **35**, **22**(61, 94); 6./StG 77: **23**(61, 94); 7./StG 77: **47**, **24**(61, 94), **76**; *Stab* 14, 47, **19**(60, 94)
Luftwaffe units, other: *Feldbataillon* 'Immelmann' 55; *Fliegerkorps*, II. 7; *Fliegerkorps*, IV. 14, 45; *Fliegerkorps*, V. 14; *Fliegerkorps*, VIII. 7, 9, 14, 24-25, 28, 34, 35, 36, 45; *Fliegerverbindungsoffiziere* ('Flivos' - air liaison officers) **71**; *Gefechtsverband Hozzel* 67, 68; *kr.S.St. 1.* (1st Croatian Ground-attack Squadron) **32**(63, 95), 85; *Luftflotte* 1: 40, 41, **43**; *Luftflotte* 2: 7, 11, 14, 25, 28; *Luftflotte* 4: 12, 14, 45; *Luftflotte* 5: 19; *Luftflotte* 6: 85; *Luftwaffenkommando Don* **66**; *Sonderstab Krim* 31, 32; *Versuchskommando für Panzerbehkämpfung* (experimental anti-tank unit) 65, 66, 69

Maahs, Fw Friedrich **76**
Macchi MC.200: **22**
Mahlke, Hptm Helmut 8, 11, 13-14
Malapert-Neufville, Hptm Robert-Georg *Freiherr* 43
Manstein, GenObst Erich von 35
Maué, Oblt 36
Mees, Ofw Otto 43
Minsk-Bialystok pocket 11-12
Moscow 25, 26, 28
Murmansk 19, 20, 37-38; Murmansk-Moscow railway 19, 20, 21, 37, 70

Nordmann, Oblt Theodor 24, 50

Operations: *Barbarossa* begins **6**, 6, 7-9, 27; *Blau* **45**, **44**, 44, 45, 51; *Braunschweig* 45; *Eisstoss* 41-42; *Götz von Berchlingen* 42; *Taifun* 24-26; *Trappenjagd* 32-33; *Zitadelle* 70-72, **71**
Orel 49-50, 69, 72
Orthofer, Maj Alfons 'Ali' 23, 48
Otte, Hptm Dr Maximilian **75**

Parpach Line 32
Paulus, Gen von 51-52
Perekop Isthmus 22, 31, 79
Pfeiffer, Oblt Johannes 20
Pflugbeil, *Gen der Flieger* Kurt 75
Platzer, Hptm Friedrich 41
Pressler, Hptm Gustav **66**

Rabben, Fw Herbert **46**

Red Army: Bryansk Front 25, 44; Group South Ukraine 80; Southwest Front 44, 45
Richthofen, GenObst Wolfram *Freiherr* von 33, 34
Rieger, Oblt Joachim 'Bulle' 28
Rohde, Oblt Hermann 72
Rostov-on-Don 23, 46, 65
Rudel, Hptm Hans-Ulrich 68, **73**, 73-74, **74**, 75
  as Oblt 15-16, 17-18, 30, 48, 53, 54, 55, **66**, 66, 67, 92-93
Rumanian Air Force 78-81, **80**; *Grupul* 3: **25**(62, 94), **78**, **79**, 79, 80, 81; *Grupul* 3/6: 81; *Grupul* 6: **26**(62, 94), 80-81
Rumanian 3rd Army 53, 54
Ruppert, Oblt Hermann 23, 32

Schairer, Hptm Hartmut 24, 49
Schiller, Maj Horst 68
Schmid, Oblt Günther **45**, 72, 93
Schmidt, Hptm Otto **47**
Schönborn-Wiesentheid, Obst Clemens *Graf* von 12, **23**
Sevastopol 22, 23, 31, **34**, 34-35, **35**, **36**, 36, 37 *see also* Crimea operations
ships, American: *Yaka* 38
ships, British: *Empire Starlight* 38; *Gossamer*, HMS 38, 39; *Lancaster Castle* 37-38
ships, Soviet: *Bezposhchadny* 22, 76; *Bezuprechny* 22, 36; *Bodry* 23; *Chervonaya Ukraina* 23; *Frunze* 22; *Kharkov* 36, 75, 76; *Kirov* 16, 17, 18, 42; *Krasnaya Armeniya* 22; *Krasny Kavkaz* 22, 31; *Maksim Gorky* 16; *Marat* 16-17, **17**, **18**, 18, 30; *Oktyabrskaya Revolutsiya* 16, **42**, 42; *OP-8* 22; *Sposobny* 21-22, 76; *Stroitel* 38; *Subbotnik* 38; *Tashkent* 36-37; *Udarniy* 22; *see also* submarines, Soviet
Slovakian Air Force **31**(63, 95); Nos 11 and 12 Sqns 84-85, **85**
Smolensk pocket 12-14
Soviet Navy: Baltic Fleet **15**, 15, 16, 41-42, **42**; Black Sea Fleet 21-22, 23, 36-37, 47, 75-76; Sea of Azov Flotilla 47
Stalin, Joseph 34, 44, 76
Stalingrad campaign **4**, 51-55, **52**, **53**, **54**, 64
Steen, Hptm Ernst-Siegfried 16, 17, 18, 93
Stepp, Hptm Hans-Karl 38, 65
submarines, Soviet: *D-6* 21, 22; *S.32* 36; *Shch-403/-404* 38

tanks **31**; *Matilda* **33**; *T-26* **11**; *Tiger* **64**
Temryuk, Gulf of 67
Teryayevo citadel **28**
Thiede, Oblt Armin **48**, 93
trains, armoured 11, 40-41, **44**, 48

vehicles **26**, **49**
Velikiye Luki 23, 24
Voronezh 44
Vyazma pocket 25

Waldhauser, Oblt Johann 33
weapons: bomb extensions, *Dinortstab* 12, **20**, **35**, **50**, **52**, **77**; bombs 7-8, 10, **16**, **21**, **25**, **29**, **48**, **49**, **50**, **53**; cannon, 37 mm 6, **65**, 65; machine gun, MG 17 7.9 mm **22**; mortar, 60 cm tracked 35
Wutka, Hptm Bernhard **71**, 72

Zemsky, Hptm Johan 52